Compassionate Leadership

Compassionate
Leadership

How to Do
Hard Things
in a Human Way

RASMUS HOUGAARD
AND JACQUELINE CARTER

HARVARD BUSINESS REVIEW PRESS
BOSTON, MASSACHUSETTS

The web addresses referenced in this book were live and correct at the time of the book's publication but may be subject to change.

Library of Congress Cataloging-in-Publication Data

Names: Hougaard, Rasmus, author. | Carter, Jacqueline (Consultant), author.
Title: Compassionate leadership : how to do hard things in a human way /
   Rasmus Hougaard and Jacqueline Carter.
Description: Boston, Massachusetts : Harvard Business Review Press, [2021] | Includes index.
Identifiers: LCCN 2021034678 (print) | LCCN 2021034679 (ebook) |
   ISBN 9781647820732 (hardcover) | ISBN 9781647820749 (ebook)
Subjects: LCSH: Leadership—Psychological aspects. | Compassion. | Wisdom. |
   Mindfulness (Psychology)
Classification: LCC HD57.7 .H6794 2021 (print) | LCC HD57.7 (ebook) |
   DDC 658.4/092—dc23
LC record available at https://lccn.loc.gov/2021034678
LC ebook record available at https://lccn.loc.gov/2021034679

ISBN: 978-1-64782-073-2
eISBN: 978-1-64782-074-9

This book is dedicated to the leaders and aspiring leaders who are committing their efforts to creating a more human world of work.

CONTENTS

Compassionate Leadership

How to Do Hard Things in a Human Way

The greatest challenge for most leaders is doing hard things in a human way.

Leaders need to make decisions that impact people's lives. They need to tell someone they did not get the promotion. They need to close an office, cancel a project, or manage an unpopular change. They need to give people tough feedback or let someone know they no longer have a job.

All leaders have to do these things that negatively impact other people. And that is hard. It is hard because we as humans are good. By nature, we want to do good, and we don't like to hurt others.

The need for doing hard things in a human way is not new. But the need for it has recently increased. Today, people in companies expect a great work experience. They expect to feel connected, to feel valued, to feel cared for and cared about. This requires leaders who are able to create a more human world of work. When leaders manage to create this experience, people thrive and perform better.

This raises an important question: As a leader, how do you do the hard things that come with taking on the responsibility of leadership while remaining a good human being and bringing out the best in other humans? In other words, how do you do hard things in a human way?

This is an eternal conundrum for all leaders. And most think they have to make the difficult, binary choice between being a good person or being a hard leader. But this is a false dichotomy. It is a terrible choice that no leader ever needs to make. Being hard and being human are not mutually exclusive. In truth, they are aligned: doing hard things is often the most human thing to do. The ability to combine these two seeming opposites comes down to one thing: wise compassion.

Wisdom is to see reality clearly and act appropriately. It is the foresightedness that comes with experience, and it helps us to deal with hard things upfront rather than beating around the bush. To have wisdom means to have good judgment in how to lead others and how to run a business in a purposeful and sustainable way. As part of our research for this book, we looked at how leaders struggle most in this regard. The answer was clear: the hardest thing for most leaders is to find the courage to enter into difficult situations with other people. Most leaders find it harder to make a decision that impacts people than to make large, strategic, and potentially risky decisions. In this regard, wisdom in leadership is about having the courage to be candid and transparent with other people and do the things that need to be done—even when it is uncomfortable. Wisdom is to see clearly that if you don't do the hard things today, they will become even harder tomorrow.

Compassion is the intention to be of benefit to others. Compassion is not about pleasing others and giving them what they want. Rather, compassion can be tough and direct, such as addressing another person's behavior if it is out of line. But it is done with the intention that helping them change will ultimately lead to better outcomes for everyone.

The Data on Wise Compassion in Leadership

As a research and consulting firm that facilitates leadership development for large companies, we at Potential Project work to create a more human world of work. As part of this mission, we have done extensive research on wise compassion over the past decade.

Specifically for this book, we have interviewed 350 executives. These have mainly been chief executive officers (CEOs) and chief human resource officers (CHROs). We focused on these two roles for a specific reason: CEOs are responsible for the most difficult decisions in an organization, and CHROs are the ones often tasked with executing them in a human way. The balance between these two is the intersection of being able to do hard things in a human way.

In addition to the qualitative interviews, we have collected quantitative data from fifteen thousand leaders and one hundred fifty thousand employees from more than five thousand companies in nearly one hundred countries. This includes two separate long-term studies in collaboration with *Harvard Business Review* and four leading business schools.[1] A particular strength of the research for this book is that we collected data from both leaders and their direct reports. This allows us to have a unique insight into how direct reports rate their leaders, rather than relying only on leaders' self-reported data.

The findings offer a strong case for wise compassionate leadership. First of all, leading with wise compassion greatly benefits yourself as a leader. Our data shows that there is a direct correlation between your own level of wise compassion and your rank in your company. In other words, wise compassion is great for your career, as it makes you rise through promotions faster. The data also found that leaders who rate themselves high on compassion have 66 percent lower stress than their less compassionate counterparts, a 200 percent lower intention to quit, and 14 percent higher efficacy.

FIGURE I-1

Wise compassion leadership data

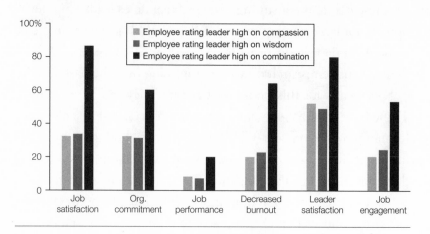

But wise compassion benefits more than yourself as a leader. As figure I-1 shows, it greatly benefits the people you lead and your organization. The graph indicates how employees rate their leaders on a scale of wisdom and a scale of compassion, then shows how these impressions correlate to how they rate their own job satisfaction, commitment to their organizations, job performance, burnout, engagement, and satisfaction with their leaders.

As the graph shows, wisdom and compassion have a significant positive impact on all aspects of the work experience and productivity of employees. An important detail to note is that when leaders combine wisdom *and* compassion, the real magic happens. The data reveals that in this case, the sum is truly greater than the parts.

The key message of our research: for optimal leadership, wisdom and compassion must be combined.

Wisdom without compassion can be ruthless, and compassion without wisdom can be naïve. Just as a bird has two wings to keep balance, wisdom and compassion must go together. You can only act truly compassionately if you also have the wisdom of understanding a situation clearly. If you don't, even your best intended actions can become a disservice for the ones you intend to support. As a matter of fact, without wisdom, good intentions can be the direct path to unskillful actions, chaos, and unnecessary human suffering for the very people you try to help.

When you balance wisdom and compassion, you have learned the art and skill of wise compassion, and you can do hard things in a human way.

The Wise Compassion Matrix

The Wise Compassion Matrix, shown in figure I-2, illustrates how wisdom and compassion need to be balanced. The matrix includes four leadership quadrants separated by two axes. The vertical axis

FIGURE I-2

The Wise Compassion Matrix

Compassion
(care)

1
Caring
Avoidance

Letting empathy or fear
be a barrier to action

2
Wise
Compassion

Courageously doing
hard things in a
human way

Ignorance

Wisdom
(courage)

3
Ineffective
Indifference

Lacking care and courage
when doing hard things

4
Uncaring
Execution

Putting results before
people's well-being

Indifference

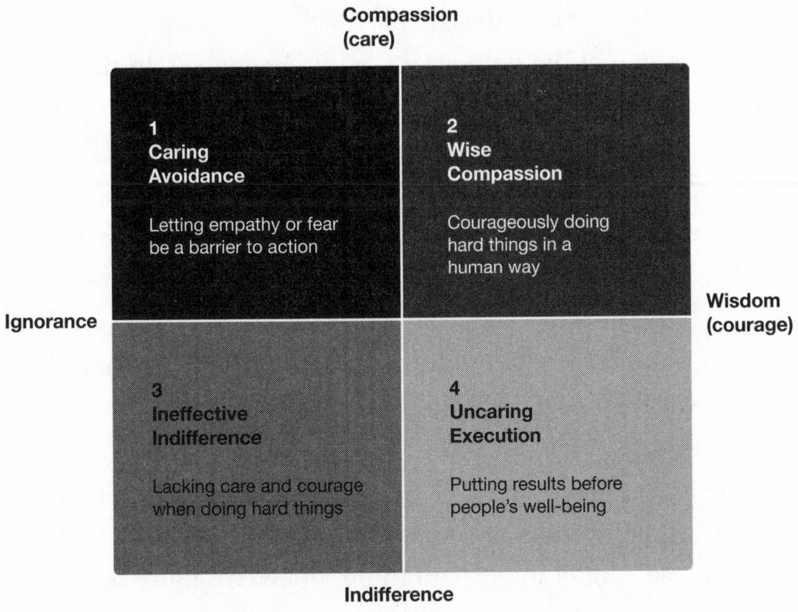

moves from indifference—or a lack of care—to compassion. The horizontal axis tracks from ignorance—or a lack of courage—to wisdom.

In Quadrant 3, at the bottom left, we're ineffective and indifferent as leaders. We can all find ourselves here from time to time when we are too busy, under a lot of pressure, or fall prey to our unconscious biases. This results in a lack of both compassion and wisdom: we can intentionally or unintentionally act in ways that are uncaring and unprofessional. Few employees will tolerate Quadrant 3 leadership. Their engagement and performance will be low, and in the long run they will seek new opportunities. Our data shows that 36 percent of leaders are rated by their employees to lead from this quadrant.

In the bottom right quadrant, Quadrant 4, we have the courage and candor to get hard things done, but our actions lack heart. We are able to drive outcomes and short-term business success, but we have little compassion. When we lead with uncaring execution, we put results before people, often at the risk of diminishing their loyalty, engagement, and well-being.

Quadrant 1, at the top left, is Caring Avoidance. In this quadrant, we care for people, but we tend to avoid the tough parts of leadership. We have a hard time giving difficult feedback or asking people to do unpleasant tasks. This can be out of fear of their reaction, or it can be out of empathy, which is different than compassion, as we will explore in chapter 3. For example, a team member is not performing well, and your responsibility is to let them know. But because you are leading from Quadrant 1 and don't want to hurt the person's feelings, you avoid providing this necessary feedback.

Finally, in Quadrant 2 (Wise Compassion), at the top right, we deliver the best results. We balance concern for people with the courage and candor to get hard things done. We move our organizations forward in an efficient and productive manner. When

FIGURE I-3

Employee experience of leadership from Quadrant 2 vs. Quadrant 3

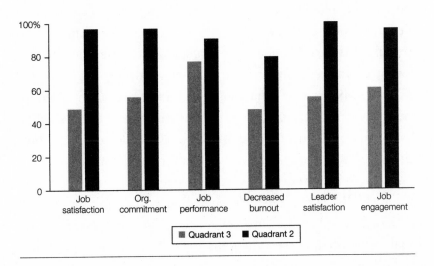

tough action is needed, we get it done with genuine care for people's feelings and well-being. Though it looks simple, this is not easy, because it goes against our neurological wiring. As humans we are wired for empathy, and it is hard for us to do hard things to others—even when it is our responsibility to do so.

There is a stark difference between the experience for followers of being led by a person seen as operating with wisdom and compassion versus those who are seen as operating with ignorance and indifference. Figure I-3 is based on our research and shows the big difference in how employees rate their job satisfaction, organizational commitment, and more, correlated to whether the leader operates from Quadrant 2 or Quadrant 3.

Clearly, the case for wise compassionate leadership is great. But it is important to note that we all operate from each of the four quadrants at different times and depending on circumstances. Based on personality and leadership style, we all have a tendency to default to one of the four quadrants. At the same time, we all move through different quadrants depending on a variety of factors, including our relationship with the person involved, our level of busyness, or the intensity of pressure we are facing. Even if we aspire to be Quadrant 2 leaders, most of us often find ourselves leading from one of the three other quadrants more often than we would like.

For example, many of us gravitate toward either Quadrant 1 (Caring Avoidance) or Quadrant 3 (Uncaring Execution) when we need to go into confrontative situations with others. In these situations, we can end up in Quadrant 1 because we do not want to hurt the person's feelings. Or we can end up in Quadrant 3 because we cannot handle the emotions we experience when doing hard things to others. Research finds that when leaders have to take difficult action, they feel guilt, shame, and anger.[2] As a result, these feelings make them shut off their emotions and compassion for the person.

So how can we avoid the traps of ignorance and indifference and operate more in the space of wisdom and compassion—the sweet spot of effective leadership?

The Wise Compassion Flywheel—Operating from Quadrant 2

Our research shows that there are four skill sets needed for a leader to operate with wise compassion when doing hard things. The first is to have *caring presence*: to be here now, with the person you are with. The second is to have *caring courage*: to choose courage over comfort. The third is to have *caring candor*, because direct is faster. And the fourth is to act with *caring transparency*, remembering that clarity is kindness.

When practiced in this order, these four skills can create a virtuous cycle that we call the Wise Compassion Flywheel. You can see this cycle in figure I-4.

FIGURE I-4

The Wise Compassion Flywheel

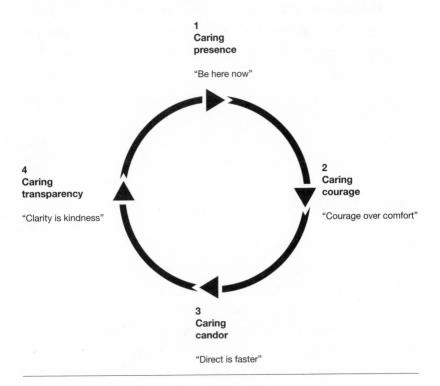

As we start to spin the Wise Compassion Flywheel, we are present when doing hard things, and we have the courage to show up with candor and transparency. When you show up in this way, it creates greater trust and psychological safety in your teams. Why? Because people know exactly where you stand and where they stand. They know you will speak your mind and that there is nothing you hold back. They can trust you and feel safe and cared for in your presence.

When spinning the flywheel, we enable others to show up with presence, courage, candor, and transparency. Over time this becomes our culture. We unleash the best in each other and cultivate happier, healthier, and more productive teams and companies.

Getting to Wise Compassion

With this book, we offer you everything we have learned about becoming a wise and compassionate leader. It is based on the best advice from the many seasoned executives we spoke with. It is based on more than one million data points from our research. It is based on fieldwork in more than five hundred companies. And it is based on the collective intelligence of everyone in our organization.

To make it easy for you, we have condensed it all into ten simple principles or mantras. The mantras are designed to be easy to remember and apply. But keep in mind that the idea of these mantras is that they are more than just words; they are concepts to be mastered so they become habitual to how we lead. This is to say, remembering and practicing them on a daily basis is what will make you a wiser, more compassionate leader. These mantras may seem deceptively simple and make intuitive sense, but they require testing, reflecting, and repeating. There is a deeper level to them all that you will only realize when you start to explore and practice them in day-to-day leadership. The following is an overview of the mantras and a preview of what's to come in each chapter.

Unlearn Management, Relearn Being Human. Wise compassionate leadership is about creating truly human connections between yourself and the people you lead. The problem with many management training programs is that they risk turning leaders into robotic managers, often speaking and behaving based on scripts and models. Chapter 1 shows you how to lead as an authentic human being to improve followership, commitment, and sense of belonging.

Great Power Comes with Great Responsibility. Wise compassionate leaders realize that they have an enormous impact on the people they lead. Therefore, when doing hard things to others, we must ensure we do them in the most human way. Chapter 2 provides guidance on leading with skillful means, reflecting on our company's purpose, and ensuring we are considering the greater good.

Connect with Empathy, Lead with Compassion. Empathy is important. It enables us to connect with other human beings. But in leadership, empathy has its downsides. We can have empathetic burnout or care so much that we avoid taking necessary action (Caring Avoidance). Chapter 3 explores how compassion is empathy plus action, and how it enables us to connect with others while also doing necessary hard things.

Your Oxygen Mask First. Many senior leaders are plagued by self-criticism and self-judgment. Research shows that that is a poor mental and emotional state for achieving excellent performance. Chapter 4 dives into how to silence the inner critic and embrace strong self-compassion as keys to leading others with wise compassion.

Busyness Kills Your Heart. We're all busy juggling many priorities. But that does not mean we have to feel busy inside. In today's fast-paced culture, being busy is a badge of honor. But busyness is a choice—and a bad choice, at that. Busyness kills our heart and thereby our ability to do hard things in a human way. Chapter 5 provides strategies for how wise compassionate leaders can recognize and avoid the busyness trap.

Be Here Now. Mindfulness enables compassion. Our research shows that the more mindful we are, the more we're capable of greater wisdom and compassion. Because of this, wise compassionate leaders benefit from cultivating greater awareness of their own mind and the mental experiences of others. Chapter 6 covers the first, foundational step in the Wise Compassion Flywheel.

Courage over Comfort. Making hard decisions often means that others disagree with you, resulting in a confrontation. Having the courage to willingly approach confrontations is one of the most important skills of wise compassionate leaders. Chapter 7 helps you develop the ability to choose courage over comfort; we examine the fear-based boundaries we need to cross to bring more courage into our leadership.

Direct Is Faster. Wise compassion is the difficult art of balancing professional candor—or directness—with personal care. We must hold people accountable while maintaining a level of compassion. This type of directness, done with care and courage, is always faster. Chapter 8 focuses on how to apply caring directness, so people receive necessary messages quickly, enabling real conversations to begin.

Clarity Is Kindness. As leaders, we need to be transparent. If not, people will not know where we stand and what awaits them. But if we are clear and open, it helps create a culture of transparency that fosters a greater sense of psychological safety. Chapter 9 covers how being transparent and clear is both a wise and a kind way to lead that, in turn, enables us to be more "here now," enabling the Wise Compassion Flywheel to spin.

The Only Way Out Is Through. In chapter 10, we reveal how to make doing hard things easy: practice. In the complex dynamics of navigating difficult conversations, the only way out is through—and by *through*, we mean through doing. By stepping into a difficult situation and coming out on the other side with a little more wisdom and a little

more compassion, we become more skillful at doing the
hard things necessary to lead in a wise compassionate way.

Each of these mantras can be read as a modular experience with
its own specific tools and techniques. There is much to be learned
by embracing each individual mantra—and you'll see immediate
improvement in your leadership practice. This means you can
jump from chapter to chapter and pull out what you need, when
you need it.

But there is an advantage to reading the chapters and embracing the mantras in order. They are designed to follow a specific
logic that builds proficiency through the understanding and im-
plementation of each one. The first five chapters help you develop
the mindsets for wise compassionate leadership. The next five
chapters (chapters 6 through 10) help you to hone the skill sets of
wise compassion. These last chapters are each a deep dive into the
individual elements of the Wise Compassion Flywheel, helping
you to lead from Quadrant 2 (Wise Compassion).

As mentioned earlier, the purpose of our research and our work
is to create a more human world of work. It is our hope that this
book will make you a catalyst in this movement. We bring its insights and strategies to you with great confidence, knowing that if
you put them into action, you will become an even better leader
who is able to do hard things in a human way.

Unlearn Management, Relearn Being Human

Nhlamu Dlomu, global head of people at KPMG, knows what it means to solve problems and manage a business. With more than a decade spent in one of the world's largest professional services firms, she has been a problem solver for many of their clients, as well as being the CEO of KPMG in South Africa. Through these years of experience, she has become keenly aware that when it comes to leadership, we often must stop our drive for managing people and instead just be human.

"As managers we always want to move fast and solve big issues," she told us. "It's coming from a good place, but sometimes we patronize and limit the very people who we're trying to develop. Our leadership would be improved by pausing to take a deep breath and asking questions of the people who we are leading. For example, asking 'What do you need?' even on decisions they may not be agreeable to is the first step before taking action."

Nhlamu's comments point to a foundational truth about the difference between management and leadership. Management is about managing others. Leadership is about seeing and hearing others, setting a direction, and then letting go of managing what happens next. If you want to be a good leader, there are a few things you need to understand: First, nobody wants to be managed. Second, who you are is more important than how smart you are. And last, leadership is all about developing and enabling meaningful and trusting human relationships.

Regardless of hierarchies and power structures within any company, we are all first and foremost human beings. We want to connect on a human level with other humans. However, many leaders have been formally trained in management skills, such as setting direction, managing plans, and solving problems. But the problem with many management training programs is that they tend to turn people into robotic managers, often speaking and behaving based on scripts and models. Although some of these tactics and skills can be helpful at times, it is important to move past them to unlearn management and relearn being human so we can show up as one human to another.

Chris Toth, CEO of Varian, put it this way: "If you start to think about what our role is as leaders, it's actually quite simple. Our role is not to be the ones who make the decision or to be the smartest person in the room. In fact, it can be exceptionally dangerous if the decision-making always goes to the leader. Instead, you must create a culture of compassion and empowerment that is accepting of diverse perspectives. This unlocks people's creativity, productivity, and happiness."

In this chapter, we look at how to unlearn management and relearn being human, starting with the need to embrace our common humanity.

Our Common Humanity

Ultimately, we are all alike. We all cry. We all get sick. We all die.

All humans have a desire to be happy and not experience difficulties. None of us wants to be unhappy or miserable. But somehow life doesn't work in a way that spares us from suffering. We all have expectations of life that are not met. We all want to be kind to others but sometimes find ourselves impatient and frustrated. We all want to feel free but end up fettered by commitments and desires for material possessions. We are all struggling to sort out our lives and our relations to others. We all do our best. And, yes, we all fall short.

This is our common humanity.

Our common humanity must inform how we lead. How we lead must change and adapt to the changes in the world, and today there is little or no separation between work and life. When work has become part of life, life has also naturally become a part of work. And when life is part of work, it brings all the emotions and feelings of life into the workplace. We as leaders must embrace this fact. For many of us, this is a new way of leading.

Kiersten Robinson, chief people and employee experiences officer of Ford Motor Company, shared that earlier in her career, she was advised not to bring emotions to work. Now, she is leading efforts to make acknowledging and understanding emotions a core part of Ford's culture and leadership DNA. She told us, "When we allow space to talk about how we are feeling and the struggles we are facing, we create a greater sense of compassion and common humanity that in turn fosters a more positive and productive work environment." For Kiersten, "being comfortable expressing and acknowledging emotions in the workplace are core elements of being human and being a great leader."

This means your role as a leader is not to check time sheets and make sure people show up on time. As leaders we must see the whole human being, not just the worker.

As leaders we are uniquely positioned to have a positive impact on others. The impact of our actions on others is amplified because of the psychological power dynamics of the leader-employee relationship. Our research show that employees who experience their leader as compassionate have 34 percent higher job satisfaction and 36 percent higher organizational commitment, are 54 percent happier with their leader, and feel 22 percent less burned out. Multiple other studies show the same results.[1] This is a massive impact in a person's life, coming from the simple fact that the leader is showing compassion.

And bringing compassion into your leadership is not as hard as you may think.

We Are Compassionate by Nature

For most of the approximately three hundred thousand years *Homo sapiens* have existed, we shared the planet with other hominoids. Around fifty thousand years ago, we prevailed while other humans died out. It wasn't because we were more populous or stronger— evidence indicates that the Neanderthals at one point were more numerous, were physically larger, and even had bigger brains. So, what happened?

In their book *Survival of the Friendliest*, Brian Hare and Vanessa Woods share the prevailing theory among evolutionary biologists that in fact our ability to care for one another is at the foundation of our survival and enduring success. They postulate that it is a "remarkable kind of friendliness, a virtuosic ability to coordinate and communicate with others that allowed us to achieve all the cultural and technical marvels in human history."[2] The underlying wisdom of caring more for each other, versus just caring for ourselves, is the foundation for collaboration, trust, and enhanced group success.

Evolutionarily, we have survived for the past thousands of years by cooperating and caring for each other. It is compassion and care that have made us the dominant species on the planet. Contrary to popular belief, our success is not because of survival of the fittest—it's because of survival of the kindest.[3] This was acknowledged by Charles Darwin when he wrote, "[It] hardly seems probable that the number of men gifted with such virtues as bravery . . . could be increased through natural selection."[4] He continued, "[T]hose communities which included the greatest number of the most sympathetic members would flourish best and rear the greatest number of offspring." According to Paul Ekman, a psychologist and pioneer in understanding human emotions, Darwin's word "sympathy" can be translated as compassion.[5]

And these theories are backed up from a neurological perspective.

We Are Hardwired for Compassion

Recent studies show that when we act in compassionate and altruistic ways, our brain and nervous system rewards us. When we show compassion for another person's suffering, it releases dopamine, leading to a sudden release of the motivational "feel good" neurotransmitter that delivers a rewarding sensation within the brain and body.[6] Oxytocin—the "love hormone," as it's commonly known—is also released when we show compassion. Its release into the bloodstream makes us feel connected and engages us in cooperative behaviors such as shared attention, eye gaze, and the dampening of the sympathetic fight-or-flight response to psychosocial stress.[7]

In short, from a neurological perspective, we are wired to be rewarded and feel good when we are compassionate. Additional research indicates that we are rewarded neurologically twice as much for "prosocial" or compassionate acts as for selfish ones.[8] In fact, studies show that it requires more cognitive effort to be selfish versus unselfish and that our natural orientation is generosity.[9]

But if compassion is in our DNA and foundational to our survival, why are we also prone to behaving in selfish, self-centered ways? Although we are hardwired for compassion, we also have default wiring that looks out for our own survival. Our ego is designed to protect us and help keep us safe, and sometimes it can get in the way of our natural ability to care about others. This can be especially true in the workplace when as leaders we are under pressure and there is so much focus on our individual performance and success.

In the coming chapters we will dive into the downsides of ego for leaders and how pressure and busyness can kill our compassion. But for now, we want to address the essence of the human versus manager debate by looking at the question of whether being a leader forces you to become colder and less kind by the nature of the role.

Does Leadership Make Us Kinder or Colder?

Many of the people we interviewed had a clear response to this question. Doing hard things does not make people kinder or colder; it just makes them better at doing what needs to be done with as much care as possible. In this way, doing hard things repeatedly over many years has the potential to transform leaders and bring them into Quadrant 2 (Wise Compassion) of the matrix in figure I-2.

Kevin Sneader, global managing partner of McKinsey & Company, described his journey to become "better" in this way: "I think you become colder and kinder at the same time. Earlier in my career, when having to deliver a hard message, I would spend my time upfront worrying. 'Oh, I can't believe I have to do this. It is going to be awful.' Now, with more experience, I am better organized and determined to be helpful. I am much better able to demonstrate caring and empathy in these difficult conversations. In some ways, you can say this makes me colder, because I am still very professional about it. At the same time, though, I can be much more human and caring because my experience helps me to anticipate what will happen and what will best help the other person."

The simple fact is we need leaders because some things are difficult to do and some problems are hard to solve. A leader is somebody who is there to be a catalyst for solving the problem or changing the situation. This is hard. And no leader we talked to said that they enjoyed doing these things. But it is part of the job—one that shapes you as a human being who potentially has greater compassion, but less individual care.

Great Compassion, but Less Individual Care

Guru Gowrappan, CEO of Yahoo, shared a framework for the different dimensions of care in leadership: "As leaders we have to operate on three levels: human-to-human, human-to-company, and human-to-society. On a human-to-human level, I have become more resolute. As a leader, one needs to sometimes be tough to help others move agendas forward. On the two other levels, however, I have become more compassionate. I care more about the greater good because I have greater ability to affect change, and with that ability comes responsibility."

In leading for a higher purpose and for the greater good, you can slowly adopt a big picture perspective on your responsibility. You accept that your responsibility supersedes the needs of individuals and has to focus on the needs of the many, on the whole organization, or even society itself. You learn to care more for the greater good, and care less for individual needs. Through repeated practice, one develops an acceptance of having to do difficult things and a tolerance to the initial discomfort in negatively impacting individual people's lives.

The Data on Wisdom and Compassion
by Leadership Level

With the above statements in mind, we gathered data on leaders' perceptions of their own levels of wise compassion, as well as how their employees perceived them. Figure 1-1 shows the results.

This figure reveals some interesting insights. First, leaders rate themselves as increasingly wiser and more compassionate as they rise in rank, with team leads rating themselves lowest, executives highest, and senior directors and upper management in the middle. Why? If we listen to the qualitative interviews, the answer is that they feel increasingly more responsibility, and therefore call for care, as they get promoted. The compassion they feel, however, is directed more to the many employees as a whole and less toward individuals.

Interestingly, this correlates logically with how their followers rate them, which is almost directly opposite. Imagine being an employee in a large company. If the executives are like Guru, Kevin,

FIGURE 1-1

Compassion and wisdom by leadership level

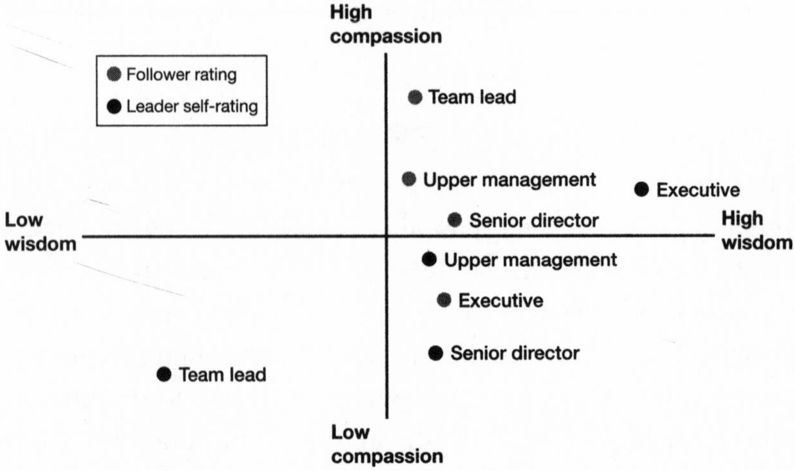

and the many others we interviewed, you may not experience a great deal of individual care from them. This is because, as they readily admit, they are focused on the greater good of *all* employees. The decisions they make may often not be the ones preferred by an individual employee. Individual employees, though, will likely rate their direct leader as more compassionate, because that person is responsible for their daily needs at work.

So, does the data show that leaders become kinder or colder as they rise through the organizational structure? Both!

This is the key: it's a choice.

In our conversation with Loren Shuster, chief people officer and head of corporate affairs of the LEGO Group, he put this choice in the context of what happens in the absence of compassion. In his view, when we do not choose compassion, we are at great risk. In his words, "We become mechanistic, lose our humanity, and that's when we start hurting each other, hurting the planet . . . it can be a pretty dark place if you choose to go there."

To enable our ability to choose to be more human and not become managerial agents lacking emotion and care, we need to develop more universal compassion.

Universal Compassion

Because many of us tend to keep ourselves too busy in our lives, our work, and our minds, compassion is often reduced to a transactional and practical element of life. It can roughly be characterized the following way: I am over here, and I am fine. You are over there and in need of help. I will help you, and in doing so I will hopefully be praised for it. Also, if things go well, you will feel indebted to me. This means I can ask a favor of you at a later time. Finally, a big reason for me to help you is that I know that I will feel better, too.

In contrast to this limited depiction of compassion, universal compassion has a much greater scope. It comes out of a universal wish for others to be happy. This type of compassion occurs when we do something good, but unexpected, for others. This type of compassion has no strings attached, no reciprocal expectations or self-serving intentions. Universal compassion comes from an inner drive to be of benefit to others.

Universal compassion is not limited to those we care for. It is not just reserved for family and friends. In truth, the compassion we have for the people closest to us is often attachment in disguise. This is an attachment to the comfort and safety they provide us through their mere existence. Universal compassion is open and expansive, and reaches out to those we find most difficult—the challenging team member, the peer who sometimes undermines our hard work, or the people from another department who are difficult to work with.

You may be asking yourself, "Why should I have compassion for a person who is hard to deal with?" The answer is simple: because of common humanity. They too want to be happy, but have struggles, just like you do. They are also someone's child, someone's parent, someone's sibling.

When faced with people who have caused you challenges, try for a moment to see things from a broader perspective. Consider that this person was born into this world as an innocent baby who grew up with expectations of a wonderful life filled with love and joy. But, of course, this person experienced the realities of life: sickness, the death of loved ones, and other forms of suffering. In all of this, despite your disagreements and challenges, you and this person are completely alike. You both want a good life, and you both experience difficulties.

When you manage to bring this broader perspective to your engagement with others, especially those who are different than yourself and those who cause you problems, you benefit greatly.

As Hugh Verrier, chair of the global law firm White & Case, said, "Compassion makes you a much better leader because it helps you see reality more clearly. When you have compassion for people who are different from you, especially when they are suffering, you see the world from their perspective, and that additional vantage point brings you closer to seeing things as they are, not as you imagine them to be." This type of compassion helps expose your biases and gives you a more nuanced perspective. As Verrier added, "Compassion also allows you to see yourself with greater insight. Compassion is what brings wisdom to leadership."

But universal compassion is not easy, especially when you must balance the needs of the business with the needs of people. These are the "rubber meets the road" moments of compassionate leadership.

Universal Compassion in Action

A leader and a company that is ready to go very far in balancing the needs of the people with the business is Gary Kelly, CEO of Southwest Airlines, the world's largest low-cost carrier. And he has a good reason to do so. For decades Southwest Airlines has been one of the most profitable airlines in the world and has been one of the fastest growing companies since it was established in 1967. In our conversations with him he shared that the core cause of the success of the company is the strong commitment to their people: "Herb Keller, our founder, said that we are a people business. Technically we may be an airline, freighting customers around the country, but the foundation of that is our people. Everything we do is done by our people. All problems are solved by our people. All happy customers are made happy by our people. If we did not put people first, they would not be able to do a great job."

Southwest Airlines, like any other airline, has been through many crises: the terror attacks of 9/11, the financial recession of 2008–2009, and most recently the Covid-19 pandemic—all of them taking massive tolls on every airline. In big crises like these, most companies choose to do rounds of layoffs to cut costs, and in the airline industry that is no different. However, since its start in 1967, Southwest Airlines has never done it. Even up to the writing of this book, it had not laid anyone off despite being nine months into the pandemic, with massive financial losses every single day. When asked why, Gary Kelly responded, "We are like a family, and you don't kick out a family member when there is not enough food. I feel a responsibility for the welfare of each and every one of our 60,000 employees." Kelly understands that a wise compassionate leader—and organization—maintains resources to weather the tough times. "The unwritten contract of loyalty between the company and our people," he said, "is the recipe for our long-term success."

It is obviously a bold move to keep all employees on payroll throughout an extended crisis. And not every company has the reserves to be able to do it. But make no mistake: it is not just a naïve decision taken from the first quadrant of the Wise Compassion Matrix. It is a decision made with the welfare of the business in mind. The conviction of Southwest Airlines is that the company can only stay successful and profitable in the long run if the unwritten contract with all employees is kept intact. It is a fine balance between the needs of each individual and the needs of the business. It is the hard art of creating a sustainable business while enabling human flourishing for everyone.

The story of Southwest Airlines is a great example of universal compassion as a company value. With universal compassion, the company is committed to the welfare of every one of its people.

But universal compassion is also an activity for any individual leader in any company. The following is a list of techniques you

STRATEGIES FOR UNLEARNING MANAGEMENT AND RELEARNING BEING HUMAN

Strategies for putting universal compassion into action so we can unlearn management and relearn being human include the following:

- Remember the Golden Rule.
- Put yourself in their shoes.
- Listen intensively.
- Always give more than you take.
- Ask yourself, How can I be of benefit?
- Stretch people to help them see their greater potential.
- Help people to see what they really need to be happy.

can use to implement universal compassion to help you unlearn unhelpful management approaches and become more human in your leadership.

Each of these techniques offers an effective step in applying universal compassion and being more human and less manager.

Strategy 1: Remember the Golden Rule

Having a compassionate intent is ultimately a genuine concern for others' well-being and a wish to alleviate or ease their struggles. Compassion, at its root, is a desire to see others happy and a readiness to take action to see it happen. To develop and express this type of compassion, the Golden Rule offers a good starting point.

The Golden Rule is a key tenet in pretty much every major religion. Often worded differently, it generally goes something like this: *Do unto others as you would have others do unto you.*

The "gold" in the Golden Rule is the reminder that we are all similar, sharing the common humanity of making mistakes,

experiencing difficulties, and facing challenging situations beyond our control. When we can see others as being "just like me,"
it enhances connection and facilitates better communication.

As Evelyn Bourke, CEO of Global Healthcare Company, shared
with us: "Treat others as you would want to be treated. Take time
to imagine what they will feel like when they hear difficult news.
Go through the emotions they will experience, so that you are
ready to embrace any reaction they may have of anger, frustration,
or sadness."

Strategy 2: Put Yourself in Their Shoes

The Golden Rule is a helpful step for putting wise compassion in
action since it requires the consideration of another person's point
of view. When we are able to put ourselves in the other person's
shoes, we can take a fresh look at a challenging situation. We can
take a moment to recognize that we have one view of the situation, but things may, and probably do, look very different from another person's perspective.

Although putting yourself in another person's shoes is good for
reflection, it is important to avoid thinking you know what the
other person is feeling or experiencing. We all want to be understood, but we don't like it when people assume they understand
how we feel or what we're experiencing. This is especially true in
today's increasingly diverse work environment. We need to balance
putting ourselves in someone else's shoes with not assuming we
understand their reality, which requires good listening.

Strategy 3: Listen Intensively

We have two ears but only one mouth. This means we can—and
should—listen twice as much as we speak. This is the case for wise
compassionate leadership. Only by listening can we understand.

And only by understanding can we lead in a way that enables success for all stakeholders.

Sandra Rivera is the chief people officer at Intel Corporation. Being the daughter of a Colombian immigrant and often the only woman in the executive suite, she has learned that listening is the best way of gaining wisdom and becoming a better leader: "Listening generously, with curiosity, without judgment, and seeking to understand is very important to having discussions when you're navigating issues that impact people. It helps us make better decisions and helps us be more informed."

Listening is the key to solving many problems both for yourself and for others. When you truly listen to others, they will feel heard and seen. Feeling seen and heard is one of our primary needs as humans. We all want to be seen and heard, not ignored or rejected. If you can listen intently, with an open mind and a willingness to learn, not only will you become wiser, but you can genuinely help others.

Strategy 4: Always Give More Than You Take

We are all searching for meaning in different ways and through different means. But while we may find different versions of meaning, there are some that are universal. We all want to do good and be good. Darwin knew it—and deep down inside, we all know it ourselves. We become happier when we do good things for other people. When we do good things that affect other people, we take part in our common humanity and in our common desire for a good life.

Yet, doing good for others can be difficult. It's hard not to think of ourselves most of the time—to think of our responsibilities, our commitments, and our challenges. But we need to get our minds off ourselves. We need to consciously decide to think of others and make a conscious decision to give more than we take.

This can be as simple as being present and giving your time to focus on others. This type of generosity is foundational for good, humanistic leadership.

Strategy 5: Ask Yourself, How Can I Be of Benefit?

A Chinese proverb says, "There is no way to compassion; compassion is the way." Asking how you can be of benefit to others is a way to compassion. Compassion is something we create by applying it to every interaction we have.

In this way, compassion can become the compass that directs your intentions, attention, and actions. Whenever you are about to engage with someone, take a moment to consider, "How can I be of benefit?" Reflect on what might be going on for this person. What is challenging or going well? And then ask yourself: What support might they need to overcome their struggles? What nudge may they need to gain more self-awareness about the blind spots that are creating their problems? What words of comfort may they need to hear from you? What tough feedback may be a compassionate nudge for them?

If you take a moment to go through these reflections before you meet people, they will experience a more human interaction, focused on their growth and development.

Strategy 6: Stretch People to Make Them See Their Greater Potential

We all want to perform and be appreciated. A good leader values who we are today but also challenges us to stretch ourselves and do better and be better to realize more of our true potential. This is not easy. When someone is already doing well, pushing them to do better can be discouraging and demotivating. But leadership is not about trying to please people and make them feel content and at ease.

Leadership is about supporting people in their development by holding a mirror and shining light on things they may not want to face. This is hard. It is hard on us because we don't want to hurt others, and it is hard on others because we are sharing things they don't want to hear. But it is precisely in these awkward, uncomfortable moments that we have the potential for growth.

A simple brain hack to help us overcome the challenge of not wanting to rock the boat is to seek opportunities to stretch people as an indication of true care: "I am hard on you because I care, because I believe in you. I know that by challenging you, I can help you realize more of your potential." Seeing your role as stretching people to realize more of their potential makes putting hard things on the table easier.

Strategy 7: Help People to See What They Really Need to Be Happy

What makes us truly happy? This is a question we all ask ourselves. And we should—it's important both for our own well-being and in helping us better lead people by understanding what drives them and makes them feel fulfilled. Regardless of how good it feels to get a pay bump or buy a new car, research tells us that external events and experiences do not create true happiness.[10] These things create pleasure, not happiness. Pleasure is merely a short-term feeling created by a hit of dopamine. As great as it can feel, this type of dopamine release can become addicting, putting us on an endless search for the next fleeting moment of gratification. True happiness, in contrast, is an experience of fulfillment and lasting well-being. It's the long-term state of experiencing a meaningful, purposeful, and positive life.

With more praise or better pay we're chasing pleasure—and hoping that it will make us happy. But it won't. This is not only true of you as a leader; it's also true of the people you lead. We all want to feel successful and enjoy the pleasure that it brings, but we need to be careful we don't mistake it for happiness. Happiness comes through our deeper humanistic experiences, such as doing purposeful work, caring for others, being generous, and making authentic connections.

When we bring more of our humanity to our leadership, we can help create a culture where others place more focus on real human connections, which creates more benefit and the potential for more genuine happiness for everyone. As leaders, we should never underestimate the impact we have on others. Because, as we will explore in the next chapter, with great power comes great responsibility.

Great Power Comes with Great Responsibility

I n 2009, multinational healthcare company Roche acquired the California-based biotech company Genentech. During years of integrating the companies, Roche decided to close its US headquarters based in Nutley, New Jersey. This was a major decision. It wasn't just its US headquarters, it was a historic site, having developed many of Roche's most iconic pharmaceutical products. But more important, the decision impacted thousands of people who would be laid off, moved to other positions, or asked to move to other locations. These were thousands of lives—thousands of families—that were being permanently changed, and even uprooted.

Severin Schwan, CEO of Roche Group, understood the magnitude of this decision. "You must understand the emotional damage of this in terms of the Roche legacy," he told us. "It was especially tough because if you close a site like this, literally thousands of people are affected." Due to the gravity of the decision, Schwan chose to fly to the site and deliver the message in person during an all-hands town hall meeting.

But there was another difficulty. To make sure that no information leaked, not a single person at the Nutley headquarters could know about the closing, including management and human resources staff. No one.

Imagine standing up in front of thousands of unsuspecting people and delivering life-changing news. But Schwan knew he needed to do it: "For me personally and as a signal to the entire organization, it was important that I didn't simply endorse the decision, but instead stood in front of the crowd and told everyone the news face-to-face." When Schwan told the crowd about the impending closing, the confusion and anger were palpable. But he knew that he had done the right thing.

Now imagine that you're preparing to tell thousands of people that their lives are about to drastically change. What would you do? It's not a comfortable question to contemplate, right? But it is a good example of the necessary evils that all leaders face. The story illuminates the importance of having a mantra to remind us that great power comes with great responsibility. This means that because leaders have formal power over the people they lead, that power must be used carefully.

As leaders, we deal with human beings. We often have power over whether they have a job or not—thus, we have control over their livelihood and their well-being and that of their families. We have power over what work they do and whether they like it or not. We also have power over how they feel treated—and this point is particularly important. Leaders have an immense—and lasting—impact on the well-being of their employees. As we shared in the introduction, leaders who lead with compassion create twice as high job satisfaction for their employees as those who lead with less compassion. Also, as our data shows, compassionate leadership positively impacts organizational commitment, job performance, engagement, and burnout.

Furthermore, research has found that if you help your people feel happy at work and enjoy an overall sense of satisfaction in life, both profitability and organizational health improve.[1] Being a good, compassionate leader is not only beneficial for employees but also favorable for the business.

In this chapter we will explore how to navigate the great responsibility for the people we have power over to ensure we are being skillful, wise, and compassionate. We will start with how this principle is amplified in hard times and can bring out the best, or worst, in our leadership.

In Hard Times, Leadership Impact Is Amplified

As leaders, we have an even greater impact on people during hard times like economic slowdowns, global pandemics, and mass layoffs. Why? Because people are anxious, vulnerable, and fearful of what may happen. During these times, people look to their leaders with a hope that they will do the right thing—even if it is hard. And if it is hard, that they'll do it in a human way.

It is during hard times that as leaders our values are tested and our true self is revealed. A crisis brings leaders' humanness to the forefront. It brings out the best and the worst in us. The best emerges when we are faced with other people's suffering. Because human beings are intrinsically good, we are compelled to exhibit compassion and care for others. The worst comes out when we fail to manage our ego's natural drive for self-preservation. When the ego takes over, we are driven by our fears of losing prestige, money, or influence. This can drive us to make decisions that are narrowly focused on our own gain. When this happens, our actions can be cold-hearted and even devastating to others.

In a crisis, great leaders stand apart from the rest through their capacity for compassion over indifference; for their sense of self-lessness over egoism. But not all leaders are up for this challenge.

Consider the example of the electric scooter startup Bird. In April 2020, as the Covid-19 pandemic started to hit North America, the valued company, valued at $2.77 billion, laid off 400 people, or about 40 percent of its workforce, through a two-minute virtual webinar. According to the people impacted by the firing, the entire process was horrible. They were invited to a call with no agenda and watched a prerecorded message with no opportunity for questions or interaction. As the call ended, the employees' computers abruptly shut down and they were remotely locked out of the company's systems. Overall, it was a heartless—and seemingly senseless—way of eliminating people's livelihood.

As we saw with Roche, firing people can be a necessity. Often, it can be the only way of saving other people's jobs and keeping an organization on track. But in firing people, you have the greatest opportunity of showing the best of your leadership skills. How? By doing it with great compassion and care. That, unfortunately, was not the case with Bird.

The example of Bird is a stark contrast to the many inspiring stories of exemplary leadership that arose during the pandemic. One that was widely shared was how Airbnb CEO and cofounder Brian Chesky handled laying off 1,900 employees representing nearly 25 percent of the company's workforce. With the company hit hard by the lack of travel during the pandemic, Chesky knew he needed to make drastic cuts to help the property-rental business weather the upcoming months—or even years—of financial uncertainty.

In addition to providing a comprehensive program for helping impacted employees find new jobs, keep their computers, retain share options, and get generous severance, Chesky's communication exemplified how to do hard things in a human way. He wrote a letter to all employees outlining what was happening, the decision-making process, and what impacted employees would receive. Most notably, the letter expressed deep compassion in a way that displayed genuine care. Chesky closed the letter with the following: "To those leaving Airbnb, I am truly sorry. Please know this is not your fault. The world will never stop seeking the qualities and talents that you brought to Airbnb . . . that helped make Airbnb. I want to thank you, from the bottom of my heart, for sharing them with us." To read the full letter, see the following website: https://news.airbnb.com/a-message-from-co-founder-and -ceo-brian-chesky/.

As a leader, guiding your organization through hard times offers a rare chance to define and exemplify who you are and what you stand for. Because of the gravity of hard times and their impact on people, your actions, good or bad, are amplified at every turn. Kind and unkind actions, however small, will be magnified. How you lead through hard times defines what people will remember about you and your leadership.

But we don't need hard times to demonstrate who you are and what you stand for. Every time you are faced with a difficult decision you can shape the nature and tone of your leadership by asking:

- Will this have a positive impact on my colleagues' genuine happiness and well-being?

- Will this action inspire others in a positive way?

- Will I be proud of this in ten years?

Let compassion be your guide now and your future legacy will take root in fertile soil. As you consider your legacy as a leader, the following are a few more questions you should consider: Are you clear on what your purpose is as a leader? How often do you reflect on your "why" as opposed to just being focused on your "what"?

What do you want to be remembered for? Do you want to be known as a leader who made the numbers or one who had a positive impact on people's lives? These questions will help you develop a true north that guides you on a daily basis and helps you when you need to take difficult action. Having this true north is always important, but even more so when you confront the necessary evils that come with the privilege—and responsibility—of leading others.

Necessary Evils

Brian Chesky's need to lay off a quarter of his workforce is an example of the necessary evils that leaders face and must act on from time to time. As a basic definition, a necessary evil is a decision we make, or an action we take, that negatively impacts others but will lead to a better result in the long term. These types of necessary evils are an unpleasant but very real side of leadership. Laying off people is a hard thing to do. But if laying off one person helps ten other people keep their jobs, then it is not morally or ethically wrong. It is simply a necessary evil—that must be done.

If you shoulder the responsibility of leadership, you are bound to have to make these types of difficult trade-offs. As emotionally challenging as these trade-offs may be, avoiding them will only make the situation worse. Necessary evils, like all hard tasks, must be confronted directly.

As leaders, part of our job is to do hard things to others in the service of the greater good. Necessary evils are aligned with utilitarianism, the ethical principle that determines right from wrong by focusing on outcomes. Utilitarianism holds that the most ethical choice is the one that will produce the greatest good for the greatest number of people.

As leaders, however, the idea—and excuse—of necessary evils must be used carefully. It is in no way a carte blanche to take ruthless or heartless actions and dismiss them as necessary evils. The litmus test must always focus on the word "necessary." Is our decision or action for the greater good? Another key consideration is our intention. What are we honestly intending with the action we are contemplating? If the intention is to serve the greater good, we are morally justified in making a difficult decision and following a hard path. If instead we are using the label of necessary evil to excuse a selfish or ego-based decision, well, we're on morally shaky ground and should reconsider our options.

Beyond the moral aspect of our position, there is another reason to be careful in pursuing necessary evils. A research study found that performing necessary evils at work may encourage employees to treat people like names on a list and deny their humanity.[2] In addition, the study found that leaders, in enacting these necessary evils, feel multiple stressors, including concern about justifiability, feelings of stigmatization, and emotional exhaustion. This does not mean, of course, that necessary evils should be avoided. The same study found that treating people with dignity and respect while letting them go—as Brian Chesky did at Airbnb— can alleviate the negative effects of difficult actions. This includes showing care, rather than withdrawing, while performing a hard task, and advocating on the harmed person's behalf. These actions not only buffer the impact of the action, but also increase positive feelings of self-worth for both the leader and the person impacted by the decision. One thing should be clear from these findings: properly handling the necessary evils of leadership requires skill.

Skillful Means

Skillful means is when you do something seemingly unkind, harsh, hard, or inappropriate to achieve a positive result for the one you do it to. The important thing is that it is done to achieve a positive result for the other, not for yourself. Skillful means is always coming from a motivation of being of benefit to the other, so in this way it is wise and compassionate.

Manipulation is the exact opposite of skillful means. Manipulation is when you do something seemingly kind to another to get good results for yourself.

Leadership, in many ways, is about applying skillful means. Mads Nipper, CEO of Orsted, the global leader in offshore wind power, put it this way: "I think leadership is fundamentally to get people to do something they would not do if the leader was not there. In this way, it could be seen as a way of manipulating. But it is only manipulation if done for my own well-being, for my own wealth. If it is done for the greater good, then it is not manipulation." Mads shared a story of skillful means with us.

In 2020 in his previous role as CEO of Grundfos, he was responsible for making a facelift to the company's 2025 strategy. He was inspired by the United Nations Sustainable Development Goals and believed that they should be part of the updated strategy. His leadership team agreed with the intention but felt it was too early to officially add them to the strategy. Mads was able to get them to agree to add a note in the presentation deck even though it was not part of the official strategy. And when the slide deck was presented internally, the commitment to sustainability was picked up by the marketing department, who convinced other leaders to make it public. In this way, by applying skillful means, Mads helped his leadership team feel pressure to take a leap and see a bigger vision for the company.

Skillful means is an important approach in wise compassion. But as it can be seen as a form of manipulation, and has the risk of being self-serving, we must ask ourselves, "How do I know that what I'm doing is right?"

Make It Skillful *and* Compassionate

Doing hard things requires foresight. Foresight helps us to lean into the unknown future and make decisions in the face of uncertainty and ambiguity. This requires reflection. Only with reflection can we have the ability to see clearly and understand that if we don't make necessary hard calls now, the future will get more difficult. As you're reflecting on what you may need to do, the three questions in the "Evaluating Skillful Means" box should be considered as a means of deciding whether your proposed action is correct.

EVALUATING SKILLFUL MEANS

To determine whether the skillful means you've chosen to pursue is wise and compassionate, ask yourself the three following questions:

- Is it selfish or selfless?
- Is it aligned with my company's purpose?
- Is it benefiting the greater good for the long term?

Each of these questions—and your resulting answers—will guide you toward making tough decisions that are beneficial to you, your team, and your organization in the long run. To help deepen your thinking, let's take a closer look at each question.

Is It Selfish or Selfless?

While we may have the best intentions of being wise and compassionate in our decisions and actions, we all have unconscious biases that shape the decisions we make. These biases put us at risk of making decisions that not only are morally questionable but also lead to poor results for the business.

FIGURE 2-1

Altruism and egoism by quadrant

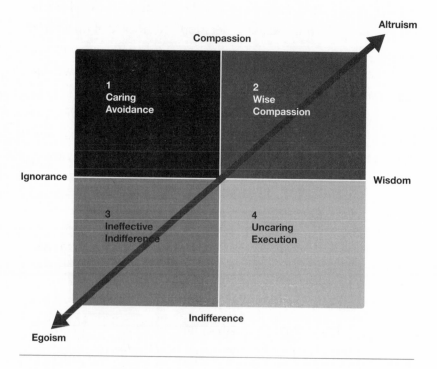

In an ideal world, we would always act with both wisdom and compassion. When we do, there is a quality of altruism in our actions. The opposite of this is when we act out of ignorance and indifference. This combination is generally ego-driven. To see how altruism and egoism fit into the Wise Compassion Matrix, see figure 2-1.

To help you better understand if you are making the right decision or taking the right action, it can be helpful to consider the role of your ego. We all have an ego. The role of the ego is self-preservation, and because it puts ourselves before others, it often influences us in ways that do not align with our values and purpose. The ego is the little voice inside our head that looks out for us first. It does this in the false belief that it is protecting us from harm. But as research experiments based on the classic prisoner's dilemma have demonstrated, a selfish individual may win in the short term but will lose in the end.[3] Instead, research shows definitively that we get the best outcomes when we cooperate.[4] Similarly, as leaders, it is in empowering and inspiring others that we create great results, not by focusing narrowly on our own self-preservation.

The ego is an obstacle to good leadership. It can easily manipulate you into thinking that what you do is altruistic, though it is in fact egoistical. It uses the idea of skillful means to tell you that what it wants is for the greater good, but its focus is self-centered.

In pursuit of self-preservation, the ego is driven by three core desires—fame, fortune, and influence. It seeks fame, believing that if you are liked, you will be safe. It seeks fortune, believing that if you have more wealth, you can buy happiness. It seeks influence, believing that if you have control over others, you can shape the world to fit your needs and desires.

Your ego steers your decisions and actions in ways that are mostly beyond your awareness. In its pursuit of fame, it drives you to seek others' approval. This, in turn, creates a likeability bias that prevents you from doing hard things. In the ego's pursuit of fortune, it drives you to make decisions that are beneficial for you in direct or indirect ways. This makes it harder for you to think long-term and more difficult to consider the greater good. Finally, the ego's pursuit of influence bends your decisions to enhance your power and status over others. None of these situations are good for you or the people you lead. To avoid being negatively guided by your ego, the following are three questions you can ask yourself before making a challenging decision:

- Will this decision positively impact my fame and how people view me?

- Will this decision positively impact my fortune directly or indirectly?

- Will this decision positively impact my influence and power in the world?

If you can answer yes to any of these questions, there is a good chance your ego is involved. In response, take time to reflect on your decision and consider how you can move away from self-centeredness and more toward altruism.

Is It Aligned with Your Company's Purpose?

Take a moment to think back to the opening story of this chapter. Why did Severin Schwan, CEO of Roche, close down the site in New Jersey, knowing it would impact thousands of employees and families? He did it because the action would support the purpose of the company, which was "doing now what patients need next." Schwan's ability to balance decisiveness with genuine concern for his employees stemmed from an unwavering focus on the company's purpose and its long-term success. "If a decision has this kind of relevance for so many people," he told us, "then you want to make sure it's worth the pain. By doing that, we can deliver better on our purpose. Can we do more for patients? Can we invest more in new medicines by having a more effective setup? By closing our headquarters in the U.S., the answer was, yes we can."

A company's purpose is its north star, its everlasting beacon that directs decisions for the long-term, greater good. But in focusing on the greater good, short-term, individual needs often must be sacrificed. And therein lies the eternal tension for any leader and any company—balancing the long-term needs of the company with the short-term, individual needs of people. By aligning your decision with your company's purpose you can guide your decision and secure greater buy-in from others.

When leaders keep their companies' purpose in mind, it eases the mental stress of making tough decisions and helps ensure that those decisions are for the greater good. As Paul Polman, former CEO of Unilever, put it: "The stronger your decision is aligned with company purpose, the easier it is to make the decisions that appear tough. We call them tough decisions, but they are often fairly obvious. We avoid them because they're not in our own interest or they don't give a short-term benefit. But when we align with purpose, the answer becomes clear."

Another benefit of aligning decisions with purpose is that it facilitates greater acceptance. If people understand your organizational purpose and see your decision as an extension of that purpose, they will be better able to accept hard things. This is especially true if you are consistent in the manifestation of your purpose—and its driving values—by attaching it not only to decisions, but to your behaviors. If you consistently marry your behaviors to a higher purpose, people will more easily accept even the most difficult change of direction or new course of action.

Is It Benefiting the Greater Good for the Long Term?

When reflecting on what it means to be a wise and compassionate leader, it is helpful to start with an examination of the role of business in society. In August 2019, 181 CEOs of America's largest companies came together in Washington, DC, to discuss this role and sign a statement about the overall purpose of corporations.[5] They brought to the meeting a shared concern about the prevailing discourse in business that the foundational purpose of a company is to enrich shareholders. The Business Roundtable, as the group is called, came together to redefine the purpose of corporations to "an economy that serves all Americans" and not just the shareholders. The statement they agreed on moved away from the idea of shareholder primacy to a recognition of, and commitment to, all stakeholders.

"This is tremendous news because it is more critical than ever that businesses in the 21st century are focused on generating long-term value for all stakeholders and addressing the challenges we face, which will result in shared prosperity and sustainability for both business and society," said Darren Walker, president of the Ford Foundation. "This new statement better reflects the way corporations can and should operate today," added Alex Gorsky, chairman of the board and CEO of Johnson & Johnson and chair of the Business Roundtable Corporate Governance Committee. "It affirms the essential role corporations can play in improving our society when CEOs are truly committed to meeting the needs of all stakeholders."[6]

This was a monumental change. With it, leaders were committing to making decisions and taking actions for the greater good, rather than just for increased dividends. But in doing so, it added new complexities to decision-making. Previously, decisions could be relatively straightforward: *How do we drive more revenue for the next quarter to meet market expectations?* But now issues like sustainability, employee satisfaction, and community well-being were explicitly included in the strategic calculus for many large organizations. Leaders soon realized that the hardest decisions are the ones they may not know were correct for years, if ever. These types of big, strategic choices take a lot of time to unwind and play out. This brought more "long-term, greater good" thinking into boardrooms, but it also helped many leaders realize a sense of responsibility as long-term stewards for their organizations. Thinking about the well-being of future generations has become a call for all leaders, even those in highly competitive, profit-driven businesses.

In January 2020, Larry Fink, CEO of BlackRock, the world's largest asset manager, with $7.5 trillion in assets under management, announced that it would put sustainability at the center of its investment strategy going forward. Among other initiatives, Fink stated that effective immediately it would stop investing in companies that present a "high sustainability-related risk." His message was clear: "We don't yet know which predictions about the climate will be most accurate, nor what effects we have failed to consider. But there is no denying the direction we are heading. *Every government, company, and shareholder must confront climate change.*" In this letter, he reiterated another core investment principle, that BlackRock will only invest in companies that put purpose at the center of their strategy. In his view, "*a company cannot achieve long-term profits without embracing purpose and considering the needs of a broad range of stakeholders.*"[7]

There you have it: "sustainability," "purpose," "needs of a broad range of stakeholders." As you consider whether your necessary evils are really necessary and your skillful means are being deployed for the right reasons, keep these words in mind. Is your decision, and the resulting action, for the long-term benefit of all stakeholders? Does it align with your organization's purpose? Is your decision selfless? If you can answer yes to these questions, you are leading with wise compassion and will have a strong, positive impact.

Before closing this chapter on great power and great responsibility, we want to address one of the key questions we explored in our research—the landscape of wise compassion as it relates to gender.

Wise Compassion by Gender

In our interviews with female executives, we asked whether they saw any differences in how women are perceived when doing hard things versus how men are perceived. We were curious whether when doing hard things, female leaders were viewed differently than their male counterparts. Many of the women we spoke with talked about being given feedback earlier in their careers that they needed to "be tougher," that they were "too emotional." Payal Sahni, CHRO at Pfizer, shared that earlier in her career she was given feedback that she should "be tougher," but rejected it because it was not authentic to who she is. She went on to explain: "Being 'tough' may sound good, but what does it really mean? For me, when you are giving feedback, it is not about you . . . it is about the person who has to receive it. Leadership requires you to think about who you are leading and your impact on them. Leadership requires trust and trust comes when people see you have their best interest at heart and are being authentic. I do what is best for the company, but in a way that is true to who I am, which means bringing compassion to whatever the issue may be."

Interestingly, in our research, female leaders rated themselves as lower on wisdom and compassion in comparison to their male counterparts, and yet they were rated as both wiser and more compassionate by their followers. In contrast, male leaders scored themselves significantly higher than they were rated by their followers. This is presented in figure 2-2.

Another interesting pattern is that women rate themselves more realistically relative to their followers' ratings. Again, in contrast, male leaders have a three-times larger discrepancy between their self-rating and their followers' ratings.

Our data also showed that female leaders instill higher organizational commitment, job satisfaction, job engagement, and job performance, and experience a lower chance of burnout for the people they lead. This was especially true for male followers of a female leader. The best leader-follower relationship in terms of performance and satisfaction is when a female leads a female. The second best is when a female leads a male. And the least productive, in decreasing order, are when a male leads a female and a male leads a male.

This data can be added to the growing body of research that contradicts outdated myths about women's ability to be strong,

FIGURE 2-2

Wise compassion by gender

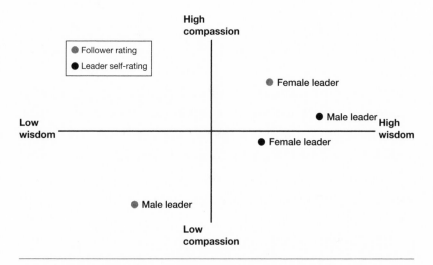

competent, tough, and highly effective leaders. It also breaks any notion that women might tend to be more compassionate and less capable of doing the hard things of leaders in comparison to their male colleagues.

In our interviews with female executives, we asked what advice they would give aspiring women leaders. The message was clear and consistent—have confidence in who you are and the value you bring to your team and organization. As Ginni Rometty, former CEO and chairperson of IBM, said in relation to advice for other female leaders: "Don't let anyone define you but yourself. Trust in who you are and have confidence in your ability to do what needs to be done."

Wise Compassion Extends to All Stakeholders

Wise compassionate leaders are ready to make hard decisions and do difficult things in a human way. This is not easy. There are many stakeholders to consider, and employees constitute just one group of constituents. As Sheri Bronstein, CHRO of Bank of America, shared with us, "It's about looking at things from every angle before you make a decision. Are we considering a balance of perspectives—our teammates, our customers, our communities, our shareholders and the future of the business—when weighing options? And then, ultimately, when we *do* have to make complex decisions, we need to practice empathy, be transparent and talk about the 'why' behind our actions in a human way."

This is what wise compassionate leadership is truly about: the ability to do hard things that are necessary, even when they are difficult. Remember, with great power comes great responsibility. And as explained in the next chapter, to navigate this great responsibility, we as leaders need to learn to connect with empathy but lead with compassion.

3

Connect with Empathy, Lead with Compassion

Tania Singer is a celebrated neuroscientist and the head of the Social Neuroscience Lab of the Max Planck Society in Berlin, Germany. She is known as one of the world's foremost experts on empathy and compassion. One of Singer's most profound discoveries came when she performed a series of brain scans on Matthieu Ricard, a well-known Buddhist monk. For the study, Ricard was strapped into an ƒMRI machine and asked to imagine the suffering of orphaned children. In previous brain imaging experiments on empathy done by Singer, this type of witnessing the suffering of others and empathizing with it activated the same affect-related brain areas as activated when feeling actual physical pain in oneself. But with Ricard, as Singer described it, "I saw networks activating that are associated with reward, like having a pleasant feeling." Singer was confounded. "What is he doing?" she wondered. "Is he thinking about lunch?"

When Singer asked Ricard about the discrepancy, he said, "You didn't ask me to suffer with these children. You asked me to engage in compassion meditation while imagining these children."

It was a true "aha" moment for Singer, as she shared with us: "I think if someone asked me what was the most insightful event of my scientific career, this was certainly one of them." In that moment, Singer had discovered an important distinction *and* relationship between empathy and compassion. First, she had discovered that the two experiences are distinct and operate through different neural networks. But she had also discovered an important relationship between them. "When you see suffering, you usually first have a natural, empathetic response. This is how you know someone needs help," she told us. "But then the important thing is that you transition to compassion. Compassion is rooted in our care and affiliation system. Evolutionarily, this is a separate system. It is a system that promotes warmth, care, altruism, and helping."

As leaders, we must connect with others through empathy, but we have to lead with compassion. Making this distinction is not just an issue of semantics: it is a critical distinction needed to secure your own well-being and the success of the people and the organization you lead.

For decades leaders have been taught the importance of empathy. And its importance cannot be overstated. Empathy is the ability to feel with another being. As a leader, this ability is obviously important. You can lead others more effectively if you can understand what they might be experiencing emotionally. Research also shows that empathy increases life satisfaction, emotional intelligence, and self-esteem. People with high empathy have larger and more fulfilling social networks, are more social themselves, volunteer more readily, donate more to charity, and are more likely to help others in need.[1]

Yes, empathy is good. But it has limitations.

Recent research into the neurology and psychology of empathy, like Tania Singer's groundbreaking study, provides a more nuanced picture, at least from a leadership perspective. Empathy has some pitfalls that every leader should understand.

In our own experience, when helping leaders understand and experience the difference between empathy and compassion, the general reaction is a deep sigh of relief. Realizing that as a leader you don't have to take on the difficulties of the people you lead is a huge burden lifted off your shoulders. Instead of carrying that burden of empathy, you can learn to experience the uplifted experience of compassion. This is a massive shift in how you engage with the people you lead, and both you and your people will benefit greatly.

In this chapter, we show you how to connect with others through empathy and how to lead with compassion. The chapter teaches you to avoid the empathetic hijack and how you can train yourself to be a more compassionate leader.

Empathy versus Compassion

Let's start by clearing up some confusion between the concepts of empathy and compassion. The words "empathy" and "compassion," as well as "sympathy," are sometimes used as if they mean the same thing. To be clear: they all represent positive, altruistic traits, but they don't refer to the exact same experience. To make a clear distinction, it is helpful to consider the two distinct qualities of compassion: understanding what another is feeling *and* the willingness to act to alleviate suffering for another. By understanding this willingness to act, we can create a chart (figure 3-1) that distinguishes compassion from empathy, sympathy, and pity.

At the bottom left, we have pity. When we experience pity, we have little willingness to act and little understanding of another's experience. We simply feel sorry for the other.

Moving up the chart, we experience sympathy. There is a small increase in our willingness to help and our understanding of the other. We feel *for* the other person.

FIGURE 3-1

Distinction between pity, sympathy, empathy, and compassion

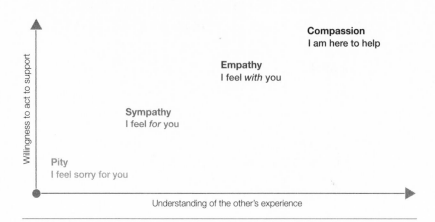

Moving one more level up, we come to empathy, where we have a close, visceral understanding of the other person's experience. With empathy we feel *with* the person. We literally take on the emotions of the other person and make those feelings our own. This is a very human and noble thing to do. However, it does not necessarily help the other person, except for possibly feeling less alone in experiencing the difficulty (more about this later).

Finally, at the top right, we have a good understanding of what the other person is experiencing *and* a willingness to act. Our understanding of the other person's experience is greater than with empathy because we draw on our emotional awareness as well as rational understanding.

Doing hard things in a human way embodies the idea that we must connect with empathy but lead with compassion. If we do not make this shift, empathy can get in the way of us doing what we need to do. Paul Polman, former CEO of Unilever, put it this way: "If I led with empathy, I would never be able to make a single decision. Why? Because with empathy I mirror the emotions of others, which makes it impossible to consider the greater good and make the right decisions. You need to have empathy on a human level but run a business with compassion."

If we lead with empathy, we end up leading from Quadrant 1 (Caring Avoidance), where we avoid taking necessary actions out of fear of hurting the feelings of others. It is a noble intention, but it leads to undesired results. If you take one thing away from this chapter, it is the following definition of compassion as a key to good leadership:

Empathy + Action = Compassion

The two terms differ in that empathy is an emotion, and compassion is an intention. Empathy is when we see someone suffer, take on the suffering they experience, and suffer together with them. This, again, is a good, altruistic response. But compassion is different. Compassion is to take a step away from empathy and ask ourselves what we can do to support the person who is suffering. In this way, compassion is an intention. As Jeff Weiner, the former CEO of LinkedIn, said: "Empathy is to see someone suffering under the weight of a great burden and respond by putting the same burden on yourself. Compassion is the act of alleviating the person from the burden."

Even from a neurological perspective, empathy and compassion are also very different.[2] As figure 3-2 shows, the brain regions activated by compassion are distinct from those associated with empathy.[3]

As you can see in the figure, empathy activates your insula and your anterior cingulate cortex. Compassion, in contrast, activates your medial orbitofrontal cortex, pregenual anterior cingulate cortex, and ventral striatum. This means that empathy and compassion are distinct neurological experiences. But beyond differences in the brain, choosing compassion versus just empathy has significant benefits for leaders and their followers.

FIGURE 3-2

Neurological difference between compassion and empathy

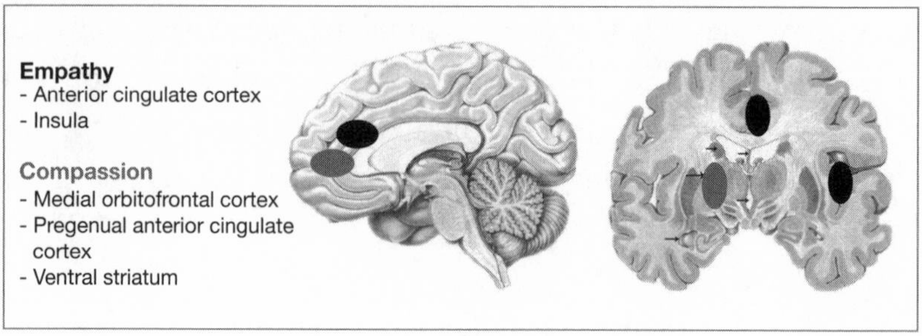

Empathy
- Anterior cingulate cortex
- Insula

Compassion
- Medial orbitofrontal cortex
- Pregenual anterior cingulate cortex
- Ventral striatum

Choose Compassion

As humans we are biased for empathy. It is deeply ingrained in our neural networks. Empathy is the natural human instinct of recognizing others' emotions and using it as a catalyst for forging bonds. Empathy kicks in by means of emotional contagion, a function of our brain's neural network that mirrors the emotional states we recognize in others.[4] When this happens, our brain mirrors the emotional state of the person we see, making us take on his or her emotions. This is a good thing. This evolutionary emotional contagion has enabled us to form emotional bonds with others and collectively form tribes that stand together in good and bad times. Without them, families, communities, and, most likely, companies wouldn't exist. For leaders with responsibility for many people's well-being, however, empathy can be a problem. The following are select benefits of compassion and potential dangers of empathy in leadership.

Compassion Makes You Feel Empowered

The data we collected for this book showed that leaders who develop and exhibit compassion over empathy in their leadership are less likely to experience personal distress or be overwhelmed by negative emotions. More specifically, the data showed that leaders with an empathy preference had a 12 percent increased risk of burnout on average compared to their more compassionate counterparts. To put this into perspective, a 12 percentage point increase in risk for burnout translates directly into an 11 percent increase in mortality risk for leaders.[5]

Another study found that compassion leads to a sense of empowerment and a predominantly positive state of mind—even in the face of other people's challenges. Why? Because compassion gives us the confidence that we can help them, rather than being caught up in their distress.[6] In this light it is not surprising that our data showed that leaders oriented toward compassion rather than empathy experience a 30 percent greater level of subjective well-being and happiness in their life in general. Also, due to their compassionate orientation, they feel a 14 percent greater confidence in their leadership ability—because they feel capable of making a difference.

Compassion Makes You Unite People

Leaders oriented toward compassion tend to focus on the greater good rather than the well-being of one individual. This means that compassionate leaders generally try to unite people and groups. Empathy, on the other hand, can make us prone to divisiveness. At its core, empathy represents our brains' evolutionary tendency to "feel with" those closest to us—those who are in our family, kin, or tribe. And when we empathize with those closest to us, those who are not close, or those who are different, seem threatening. In their book *Survival of the Friendliest*, researchers Brian Hare and Vanessa Woods explain that our unique ability to care for one another comes at a cost: "Just like a mother bear is most dangerous around her cubs, we are at our most dangerous when someone we love is threatened by an outsider." Their research reveals how our ability to have empathy makes us "the most tolerant species on the planet and also makes us the cruelest."[7] In fact, recent research finds that people prone to empathy are also prone to enjoying seeing other people (those who are not part of their in-group) experience problems.[8]

Because of this, studies have found that empathy can also lead to a lack of diversity and inclusion.[9] As mentioned, humans empathize more easily with people similar to themselves. Even other animals that resemble humans receive more empathy. Just think of a baby seal with its big, round eyes, as opposed to a chicken. Which would you more readily kill and eat? Similarly, we easily empathize with a neighbor whose car is stolen and less easily with the homeless person on the street. In much the same way, we unconsciously empathize with colleagues who are similar to us. We tend to offer them better assignments and better positions, all unknowingly. This can create an organization that suffers from lack of diverse perspectives, limiting problem-solving, innovation, and creativity.

Our data showed that leaders who are orientated toward compassion over empathy are better for the team. Our assessment measured how leaders scored on the empathy versus compassion scale and then correlated that with how employees rated their leaders and their own experience of work. The followers whose leaders show a compassion preference are 25 percent more engaged in their jobs. They are also 20 percent more committed to the organization and have an 11 percent lower risk of burnout.

Empathy Can Lead to Immoral and Unethical Decisions

Even with its many benefits, empathy can be a poor moral guide. Yes, you read that correctly. Empathy often helps us do what's right, but it also sometimes motivates us to do what's wrong. Research by Paul Bloom, professor of cognitive science and psychology at Yale University and author of *Against Empathy*, discovered that empathy can distort our judgment. In his study, two groups of people listened to the recording of a terminally ill boy describing his pain. One group was asked to identify with, and feel for, the boy. The other group was instructed to listen objectively and not engage emotionally. After listening to the recording, each person was asked whether they would move the boy up a prioritized treatment list constructed and managed by medical doctors. In the emotional group, three-quarters of participants decided to move him up the list against the opinion of medical professionals, potentially putting sicker individuals at risk. In the objective group, only one-third of the participants made the same recommendation. This study demonstrates how empathy triggers our impulses, resulting in poor judgment that could harm many people for the benefit of one person. As leaders, empathy may cloud our moral judgment. It encourages bias and makes us less effective at making wise decisions.

With all these challenges of empathy in leadership, one may think it should be completely avoided. That, however, is far from the case. A leader without empathy is like an engine without a spark plug—it simply won't engage. Empathy is essential for connection and then we can leverage the spark to lead with compassion.

Empathy Is Needed—but Just for a Moment

Both empathy and compassion are fundamentally important in leadership, but although compassion will support your leadership all the time, empathy should only be used as a springboard to catalyze compassion. And therein lies the challenge for most leaders: we tend to get stuck in an empathy trap and not move into compassion.

"I have a bias for empathizing with human beings," Mads Nipper, CEO of Orsted, the world's most sustainable energy company, explained to us. "I think that has enabled me to forge good and trusting relationships throughout my career. But the downside is that I sometimes find it hard to make difficult decisions that impact others. I have to force myself to get out of the connection of empathy and actually do what needs to be done to serve the bigger purpose of our company."

Mads's experience is similar to that of the vast majority of leaders we have worked with over the years, as well as those we have interviewed for this book. Our natural human inclination is to have empathy for others. This is Quadrant 1 (Caring Avoidance) leadership. Moving into Quadrant 2 (Wise Compassion) means making a conscious choice and takes effort.

This does not mean we should abandon empathy.

Leverage the Spark of Empathy

Empathy is the emotional spark that ignites our compassion. In this way, empathy is our gateway from Quadrant 1 to Quadrant 2 leadership. Instead of being caught in an experience of empathy, we must learn to use it as a spark to move into action. This is how we avoid the "empathy trap" of taking on others' suffering. In this sense, empathy becomes a catalyst rather than a tool in itself.

Figure 3-3 shows this experience of choosing compassion over empathy once we've experienced the initial spark. In the figure, you meet a colleague in distress. Seeing their suffering, you experience an emotional contagion—empathy. And from here you have to make a decision: Will you linger in their suffering and be empathetically hijacked? Or will you move into the intention of compassion and act to alleviate their distress?

Because of our bias for empathy, it's natural for us to stick with empathy. Due to our neural wiring, it is comfortable and natural

FIGURE 3-3

The spark of empathy

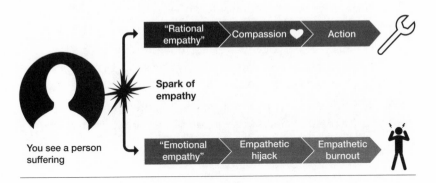

to do so. But as leaders, we need to move out of this state and into compassion by taking a mental step away from the person, putting the situation into perspective, and then asking, "How can I help?" We do this by not dwelling on our sense of empathy, but instead using it as a lever to awaken our compassion.

It is important, though, to avoid making this a robotic shift. We must show the person that we have felt what they feel. When they believe that we've seen them and understand what they're experiencing, we can establish emotional resonance. This creates trust, and trust opens the other person to receive help. But to do this, we first must overcome the empathetic hijack. Before we explain how to overcome this hijack, let's take a moment to experience the difference between empathy and compassion.

Experience the Difference between Empathy and Compassion

It is good to have a conceptual understanding of the difference between empathy and compassion, but to truly comprehend the difference, it is important to experience it. Experiencing it is a key

EMPATHY VERSUS COMPASSION

Ten steps to experience the difference between empathy and compassion:

1. First of all, close your eyes and sit comfortably. Take a few moments of just relaxing your body and mind. Let go of anything you have just read.

2. Now bring to mind a person you really care about and who has, in recent times, experienced significant suffering either emotionally or physically.

3. Imagine this person sitting right in front of you.

4. Try to notice how the suffering they have experienced or are experiencing is showing up in their facial expressions and maybe even their body language. Sit and take it in for a few minutes.

5. If by now you are feeling a slight or strong sense of heaviness or sadness, this is the experience of empathy. This is good. It means you care.

6. But to really help the person, you need compassion. To get to this, move to the next step.

7. Imagine you are taking a few mental steps away from the person, to get some perspective. And then ask yourself, "How might I be able to help this person?" What small or big thing can you do to make them feel a little better? Can you give them a call, send a text, pay a visit, or send a gift?

8. Make a strong commitment to yourself to do at least one thing to help the person. Sit with this commitment for a few moments. Recognize that you are in a position, even in a small way, to make a difference for this person and help them with their challenges.

9. How do you feel now?

10. If you feel slightly lighter than earlier, this is the experience of compassion: the intention to do something to help another in need and the understanding that you have the power to make a positive difference.

step in learning to overcome empathetic hijacks. The "Empathy versus Compassion" box describes a simple exercise to help you experience the difference firsthand.

Empathy versus Compassion by Gender, Level, and Industry

As part of our research for this book, we took a deep dive into the demographics of leaders leaning toward empathy or compassion. This study yielded some interesting findings about gender, level of seniority, and industries. Figure 3-4 shows our findings.

One interesting, and perhaps not surprising, finding is the distribution of seniority level along the spectrum. On the empathy orientation of the spectrum, we have the more junior roles of staff and team leads. As we move toward the compassion orientation, we have middle managers, then upper management, then senior directors, and finally executives. Only 6 percent of executives did not score strongly on the compassion orientation.

This data correlates with our qualitative interviews where leaders shared with us the importance of focusing on the greater good—

FIGURE 3-4

Empathy vs. compassion by gender, level, and industry

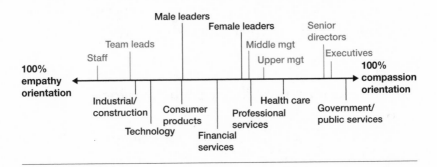

the entire organization and beyond—rather than zooming in on each individual. As you rise in rank and your responsibility widens, you are forced to take a bigger perspective and hopefully be more oriented toward compassion. If you cannot do this, you will likely not be successful in filling the role. Also, with an increased responsibility for more people, if you don't move away from empathy for the individual, you may risk suffering from empathetic burnout.

The figure also shows the distribution of industries along the spectrum. We see government leaders strongly oriented toward compassion. This makes sense in that government and public work is defined by being in service for the greater good. On the other end, we see technology. An explanation for this may be that technology as an industry is still relatively young compared to other industries. Also, it is an industry with many relatively young leaders who may not have yet embraced the wisdom of compassion.

Finally, the figure shows that women, more than men, are generally oriented toward compassion over empathy. This makes sense given the data in the previous chapter about women being rated as more compassionate than their male counterparts. It also resonates with our data showing that females lead in a way that creates greater job satisfaction, job performance, and job engagement. If as leaders we are oriented toward empathy, we will tend to hold people less accountable, stretch people less, and not share hard feedback. And when we avoid doing those things, we damage trust. This, in turn, leads to poor job satisfaction, performance, and engagement. To avoid this fate, we must learn to overcome the empathetic hijack.

Overcoming the Empathetic Hijack

As we discovered earlier in the chapter, the feeling of empathy can be seductive. When we empathize with a person or a cause, it can create a strong feeling of being right and doing the right thing, just like righteous indignation, loyalty, honor, and pride. The moment we experience these feelings, it can feel good and in line with our values. They make us feel like we're standing up for the right thing. In this way, the feeling of empathy can be addictive.

Overcoming this empathetic hijack is an important skill for any leader. And it is a skill that is very possible to learn. In mastering this skill, it is important to remember that shifting away from empathy does not make you less human or less kind. Instead, it makes you better able to support people. The following are strategies for using empathy as a spark for leading with more compassion.

- **Take a Mental and Emotional Step Away:** When you are with someone who is suffering, to avoid getting caught in an empathetic hijack, try to take a mental and emotional step away. Step out of the emotional space to get some perspective on the situation and the person. Only with perspective will you be able to help. Taking a step away may feel like you are being unkind by not being in it together. But remember this is the luring trap of empathy. Remember this will not necessarily help the person. By stepping away, you are not stepping away from the person. You are stepping away from the problem so you can better see it in perspective and help solve it.

- **Ask What They Need:** The first step toward being helped is to feel heard and seen. When you ask the simple question "What do you need?," you have already initiated the path to solve the issue by giving the person an opportunity to reflect on what might be needed. Their response will also inform you better on what you can do to support them.

- **Establish Emotional Resonance:** Remember that humans in pain are looking for recognition from other humans who know what they are feeling. Forget about your managerial status and be a fellow human on the path of common humanity. Don't fall in the trap of moving into solutions mode before having established the emotional resonance that happens when the other person feels you have actually seen and heard them and that you are there to help.

- **Coach the Person to Find Their Own Solution:** Leadership is not about solving problems for people. It is about growing and developing people, so they are empowered and get skills to solve their problems better on their own. Avoid taking this life-learning opportunity away from people by solving their issues. Rather, coach and mentor them to find their own answers to their challenges.

- **Remember the Power of Nonaction:** Leaders are generally good at solving problems and getting stuff done. That's why they were promoted in the first place. But when it comes to people having challenges, it is very important to remember that often people don't need your solutions. They just need your ear and your caring presence. Many problems don't need a solution, but rather to just be heard and seen. Not acting on others' problems can oftentimes be the most powerful way of helping.

Compassion and Self-Care

When we empathize with a colleague we care for, it feels nice. It makes us feel that we're good because we take part in the suffering of others. But this feeling is a trap. Because it feels right, empathy can be alluring. When we as leaders repeat this pattern of applying empathy, it becomes our default way of dealing with other people's suffering. For leaders who manage multiple reports, this can be a danger due to the risk of taking on many people's suffering and experiencing emotional exhaustion. And just because the emotion of empathy feels right doesn't mean that our resulting actions are positive, constructive, or wise. As we've seen throughout this chapter, the opposite is often the case. Instead, we need to approach hard decisions and actions with a sense of compassion, the combination of empathy and action.

But even if we, as leaders, face difficult situations with compassion—with the skill and discipline to stand back, judge objectively, and act accordingly—we still face the possibility of emotional exhaustion. In truth, no matter how we define it, the task of absorbing, reflecting, and redirecting the feelings of other people can be overwhelming. Because of this, as leaders shouldering responsibility, we must practice self-care. We need to find ways of staying resilient, grounded, and in tune with ourselves. When we show up in the workplace with these qualities, people can lean on us and find solace and comfort in our well-being. In the next chapter, we take a deeper look at the emotional costs of leadership and provide helpful strategies for self-compassion and self-care.

Your Oxygen Mask First

A number of years ago, Jesper Brodin, CEO of Ingka
Group, IKEA, faced a difficult situation. He had been
asked to take over responsibility for managing IKEA in
China. After some months of analysis and reflection, he and the
team came to the conclusion that the business was overly complex
and needed simplification to be successful. Significant changes
would have to be made in the short and midterm to ensure a strong
business for future generations. These included closing offices
which would require supporting a significant number of employees to find new employment. In a people-centered organization
and business such as IKEA, where employees are valued like family,
this was a difficult situation.

But another question was also on Jesper's mind, a question that
needed a clear answer before engaging in such a big and difficult
restructure. The question Jesper was asking himself was, "Do I,
and we, have the courage and stamina to do this?"

Though it may seem like a simple question to answer, it is a very
important one. As Jesper shared with us, "As a leader instigating a
long and difficult process, you have to make sure you are up for it.
You have to make sure that you are ready to work long hours for

months. Because if you are not, and only discover your limitations at the halfway point, you will do irreversible damage to your people, to yourself, and to the business. Professional and caring, that becomes the motto for us leading the change; professional to do what is right in the right way and make sure we are human and present in all parts of the journey."

When we think of good leaders, we imagine people who are visionary, decisive, calm, clear, and confident. We don't always see what it takes behind the scenes to bring these qualities to the forefront. In Shakespeare's play *Henry IV, Part 2*, his lead character laments, "Uneasy lies the head that wears a crown." In our discussions with C-suite executives, we invited them to share their "uneasiness." We did this to help shine some light on the harder sides of leading others. Not surprisingly, they all shared that it can take its toll on those who need to make tough decisions and have difficult conversations.

In fact, we heard from a number of leaders that if they don't feel the weight of the impact their decisions have on people, they would be concerned. So how do leaders deal with the pressure and discomfort of doing hard things to other human beings? By putting on their own oxygen mask first. In other words, when we have the wisdom to be compassionate to ourselves first, we enhance our ability to lead others.

This was evident in our data from a survey of global leaders. We found that leaders who rated themselves higher on compassion also reported 63 percent lower burnout, 66 percent lower stress, and a staggering 200 percent lower intent to quit their organization. Highly compassionate leaders also felt more confidence in their own ability to lead others and reported being on the same page as their followers more often.

In another assessment of over fifteen thousand global leaders, we found a correlation between self-care and rank.[1] The more senior the leaders, the more they reported better self-care in terms of getting enough sleep, exercising regularly, and other healthy habits. At first, we thought this was only people at the very top of the organization—those who had teams of people to take care of things like emails, scheduling, and meetings. But in looking deeper at the data, we found a pattern. The data indicated that as people rose in rank, their reported self-care increased.

To be a wise and compassionate leader, it is imperative that we are up for the task; that we have the courage and strength to do hard things in a human way. Only when we have wisdom and compassion for ourselves can we truly have wise compassion for others. Just as they advise on airplanes, before you can help other people you need to put your own oxygen mask on first. Only when we are okay can we help others to be okay.

Being a leader requires making tough decisions. Making tough decisions means negatively impacting other human beings. As we have explored throughout this book, we are compassionate by nature and don't like to bring harm to others. Therefore, being a leader means doing harm to others—which is difficult because it doesn't come naturally. Successful leaders have recognized this and have developed strategies to ensure they take care of themselves. This is not just a list of "shoulds." For leaders who understand the "weight of the crown," self-care is wisdom. Leaders who do not have the wisdom to take care of themselves will either burn out or simply be lousy leaders.

In this chapter, we will look at some of the most common challenges leaders face in doing hard things to others from an emotional and social perspective. We will then explore strategies for self-care and self-compassion directly related to navigating the "hits" associated with doing hard things.

Loneliness, Sadness, and Doubt

Leadership is often viewed as a prize, a sign of status, an indication of achievement. And it is. Few rise up the ranks without a demonstration of skill and competence. But the "prize" comes with costs. It is not easy to bear the weight of tough decisions, especially those that impact the lives of other human beings.

One of the questions we asked the leaders we interviewed was, "What impact does doing hard things have on you?" The responses ranged from "It's tough" to "I hate it." We are inherently good. We don't want to cause harm to others. Doing hard things is hard, and it takes a toll. For the leaders we interviewed, the three most common tolls or costs of doing hard things were loneliness, sadness, and doubt.

Loneliness

One of the most common challenges shared by C-suite executives, and particularly CEOs, was loneliness. A sense of loneliness becomes even more pronounced as you reach the higher ranks in an organization. With each progressive leadership role, there are things you know you can't share with others and decisions you need to make that will negatively impact people you care about.

Evelyn Bourke, the CEO of international healthcare company BUPA, said, "It can be a very lonely job to be CEO, especially when having to make hard decisions. You can't relate to your colleagues in the same way as they can to each other because you are their boss. As much as you engage others, being in charge often means you are very much on your own, carrying the burden of hard decisions."

This feeling of isolation makes sense. As leaders, there are times when you have to make decisions that create dissent, disagreement, and distance. Especially with "big" hard decisions. There will be times when you are separated from your colleagues and from members of your leadership team. So, loneliness in many ways is natural, understandable, and "to be expected" as a leader of others.

But it doesn't mean it is easy.

We are social beings. From a neurological perspective, one of our greatest fears is being alone. When we experience isolation or being ostracized by the group, it threatens psychological needs of belonging and negatively impacts physiological functioning.[2] Deeply rooted in our ancestral brain is the profound awareness that we cannot survive on our own. As social beings, we thrive through feelings of connection and intimacy with others.[3] To be successful as leaders, it is important that we have people we can share things with. For many of the leaders we spoke with, the person they engaged to overcome the sense of loneliness and isolation was their partner or spouse. But it could also be a peer, a close friend, or a trusted colleague. The key is to recognize the reality of the natural loneliness that comes with the role and ensure you have someone you can talk to and feel a sense of true connection.

In this light, it is not surprising that research finds that many successful and high achievers tend to have higher levels of social support from various relationships. They're high achievers in the first place because they make sure they aren't alone in achieving those milestones. Being successful and performing well in one's life or profession isn't a lone wolf thing. It takes the tribe around you to build your strength and motivation to pursue future successes.[4]

But often when leading others, and specifically when making tough decisions, we are on our own. That's just the way it is. It is one of the costs of carrying the weight of leadership. We may have others we can ask for input and advice, but if we are in charge, we are left to weigh the options and determine the best path forward. This can be lonely and sad.

Sadness

One of the questions we asked all of the leaders we interviewed was, "What is one of the hardest things you have had to do as leader?" The answer: Making decisions that negatively impact people. This shouldn't be a surprise. Our connection to people is naturally stronger than our connection to machines, buildings, or locations. As Mads Nipper, CEO of Orsted, told us, "I can make huge financial decisions, like billions of dollar investments. And do it very calmly. I can sleep well at night. But when it comes to making difficult decisions about people, I feel sad and uneasy. Those are the decisions that create anxiety."

As leaders shared stories about really tough situations, there were moments in a number of interviews when there were tears. It was clear that these stories—these events and decisions—still darkened their thoughts. Even in cases when the outcomes were positive, when the decision led to higher performance or continued success, these leaders still felt strongly for the people who were affected. This helped us realize an important truth: all businesses are people businesses. It just doesn't matter how much money you move or how many strategies you alter, it will always be the people you affected that will impact you the most.

When we accept a leadership position, we don't think about the fact that we will have to make decisions that negatively impact people's lives. But this is part of the role. And although sadness is tough, sadness is a good teacher. The imprint of sadness ensures that we don't lose sight of the impact of our decisions on other people. In this way, the lasting imprint of sadness is a good thing. Feeling miserable means we are still connected with our humanity. If we don't feel sad when doing hard things to others, we should be worried.

When we spoke with Lucien Alziari, CHRO of Prudential Financial, he said that if he ever went home after having communicated a tough decision and did not feel miserable, he would be concerned that he had "lost the plot." At the same time, he uses these feelings to ensure that people are being treated fairly and with real empathy. As he shared, it is "healthy and human to be sad knowing there is a human being on the other side of that decision who has to go home and deal with the consequences." He sees this as a good way of calibrating whether the decision still makes sense in the larger context of the whole organization.

Doubt

The third toll that doing hard things can have on us is a sense of doubt. How do you know that you are making the right decision? Doubt comes as par for the course in rising up leadership ranks. If the answer was obvious, someone else would have made the decision, and it wouldn't have landed on your desk. Every leader we spoke with shared some version of how they wrestled with tough decisions, struggling with not knowing for sure the right path forward. And the more senior you get, the bigger the impact of your decision and the less clarity there is on whether it will turn out the way you expected. Even after a decision was made, many leaders spoke about a lingering feeling of doubt.

Doubt is a tough emotion for leaders. We look to leaders for clarity, for decisiveness. When we are in doubt, we look to leaders for certainty. We want our leaders to make the tough decisions and show confidence that they chose the best path forward.

But like sadness, doubt can be a good reminder of the impact leaders are having on human beings. If we didn't pause for a moment of doubt before doing something really hard, we could be at risk of arrogance and insensitivity. Doubt keeps us connected and enables us to bring natural humility to the reality of the task at hand. The key is to allow doubt to arise, but not let it fester. Successful leaders are the ones who can use insights from their doubting minds and move forward.

Taking Care of Self

If you want to be a wiser and more compassionate leader, you need to start with bringing wisdom and compassion to yourself. You can only have the capacity to take care of others when you are healthy and strong. When you bring wisdom and compassion to yourself, you're able to recognize the emotional signs of stress and develop coping skills to manage them. Having an awareness of your own wellness and well-being also helps you sleep better and have more meaningful relationships with those around you. And, of course, it helps relieve many of the issues mentioned in the previous section.

In our previous book, *The Mind of the Leader*, we shared a number of strategies for taking care of self. One of the most basic and most important is getting good sleep. We won't repeat all of the background and strategies here, but the bottom line based on extensive research is that you are not the best version of yourself without sufficient rest. No one wants to work for a grumpy boss. When you are tired, you are more likely to do hard things poorly.

But beyond basic self-care, which also includes exercise and good nutrition, we want to focus in this chapter on strategies to put your own oxygen mask on first specifically related to the challenges of doing hard things. These strategies are befriend the inner critic, beware the second arrow, and recharge your batteries.

Befriend the Inner Critic

Many people become leaders because they are high achievers and have been promoted on that basis. This is good, but it often comes with a downside. High achievers are generally good at pushing through a challenge regardless of their own boundaries or limitations. Also, high achievers are successful because they can be relentless in improving themselves through inner criticism.

And although inner criticism can be a wise teacher, it can also be a terribly unkind and unhelpful friend. But how to know the difference? How to distinguish the voice that helps guide us toward more wise decisions versus the voice that can crush our confidence? The difference is the application of wise compassion to self. In this book we have shared many ways to show compassion to others. When navigating the inner critic, the key is to bring that same level of compassion to ourselves. Pay attention to how you talk to yourself. When you find that you are too critical toward yourself for something you could have done differently, ask yourself, "Would I talk to a good friend in this way?"

One of the obstacles in facing and managing the inner critic is that sometimes it points out something that has an element of truth. And because we know it is a weakness, we let the inner critic bash us all day. This type of self-judgment can go on for days, or even months, after the event has passed. But the fact that something is true does not justify our critic using it as ammunition to undermine our own self-worth. It does not warrant the critic harassing us dozens of times a day.

The internal critic's rationale is that if it gets on your case enough, you will stop making mistakes, messing up, forgetting things, or causing yourself embarrassment or trouble. Chastising someone, however, is rarely a good motivator for correcting habits or eliminating mistakes. It just makes you feel bad.

Would you let a friend or partner walk around all day telling you all the things you have done wrong? Probably not. You would say, "You told me that once before, and I get it. I plan to address it. Now drop it and leave me alone. You don't need to keep reminding me." You can employ a similar strategy with your inner critic. With a simple acknowledgment you can tell the critic, "Yes, I heard it the first time. I got it, thanks. I don't need to hear this anymore."

The key to working with the inner critic is to be able to recognize it when it arises. Do you know what your inner critic's voice sounds like? Do you recognize common situations during which it is more likely to show up? This requires an ability to create distance between you and the narrator in your mind so you can be more objective about your thoughts. From this vantage point, you can apply some wisdom: "Is this helpful to me right now?" Or "Is this accurate or is there another way of looking at this situation? Is there a bigger picture?"

The antidote to self-criticism is self-compassion. Kristen Neff, professor at the University of Texas and author of the bestselling book *Self-Compassion*, puts it this way: self-criticism asks, "Am I good enough?" Self-compassion asks, "What's good for me?" in terms of my own mental health and well-being. The number one reason people give for why they aren't more self-compassionate is the fear that they will be too easy on themselves. Without constant self-criticism to spur themselves on, people worry that they may lose their drive and slack off. They see self-compassion as the same thing as self-indulgence. But is self-criticism really the great motivator it's cracked up to be?

Research shows that self-critics are much more likely to be anxious and depressed—not exactly get-up-and-go mindsets. They also have lower self-efficacy beliefs (i.e., self-confidence in their abilities), which undermines their potential for success. The habit of self-criticism engenders fear of failure, meaning that self-critics often don't even try achieving their goals because the possibility of failure is unacceptable. Even more problematic, self-critics have a hard time seeing themselves clearly and identifying needed areas of improvement because they know the self-punishment that will ensue if they admit the truth. It's much better to deny there's a problem or, even better, blame it on someone else.[5]

The voice and narrative in our heads are often the only things that stand between us and our success. Kristen Neff said, "Self-compassion involves being kind to ourselves when life goes awry or we notice something about ourselves we don't like, rather than being cold or harshly self-critical."[6]

There is a subtle but important difference between an inner critic, which sometimes can have good insights for us, versus when we are just letting negative thoughts fester. The harsh critic can help us learn from an experience: "Next time I will try to do that a little differently." This type of self-reflection, though difficult, can be useful. But the mind that ruminates on a negative experience without adding any value is why we need to beware of the second arrow.

Beware the Second Arrow

There is an old Buddhist parable of the second arrow. The Buddha once asked a student, "If a person is struck by an arrow, is it painful? If the person is struck by a second arrow, is it even more painful?" He then went on to explain, "In life, we cannot always control the first arrow. The second arrow, however, is our reaction to the first. It's important to remember that these second arrows—our emotional and psychological response to situations—are natural and very human. But the truth is, they often bring us more suffering by cluttering our mind and keeping us from seeing the best course of action. With this second arrow comes the possibility of choice."

In other words, the first arrow causes unavoidable pain, and our resistance to it creates fertile ground for all the second arrows. The way to overcome this natural tendency is to build our mental resilience through learning to understand and manage our mind. Mental resilience, especially in challenging times, means managing our minds in a way that increases our ability to face the first arrow and to break the second before it strikes us.

Kathleen Hogan, chief people officer at Microsoft, shared her experience of a second arrow when she received negative employee feedback during an employee all-hands meeting. Someone reacted to Kathleen's response to an employee question and shared this comment in the chat: "Kathleen gets an F as the head of HR for that." Kathleen initially took this comment to heart, especially since she strives to be an A student for employees (or at the very least a B). She believed that Microsoft was focusing on the right things and that in a company with over 160,000 employees globally, she recognizes not everybody would agree with her decisions. Part of being a leader is accepting positive and negative feedback and activating a growth mindset to reflect, learn, and move forward, and try to not let it bother you.

A good approach to dealing with second arrows is talking with others and getting diverse perspectives. For Kathleen, she reflected on advice from her manager, Satya Nadella, the CEO of Microsoft, who encouraged her to "zoom out" and "look for the signal amidst the noise." Instead of focusing on the negativity of the comment, seek to understand what the individual was trying to convey and focus on the learnings and ideas for future improvement.

Acceptance is the ability to not make a bad situation worse. In doing hard things that affect people, we will experience adversity and challenges. Our ability to accept, rather than reject, is the difference between inner peace or long and exhausting inner battles. We talked with the Dalai Lama about leading during difficult situations. He shared something he is often quoted for: "If you have a problem and you can do something about it, what reason is there to worry? But also, if you have a problem and you can't do anything about it, what reason is there to worry?" Rejecting situations that are challenging only makes them stronger. The path to inner peace is acceptance. Acceptance is the skill of noticing our own thoughts, unhooking from the unconstructive ones, and rebalancing quickly. It is recognizing that being a leader means doing hard things, and doing hard things requires letting go. It requires being aware and letting go of the second arrows.

But keep in mind, letting something go is not the same as letting yourself off the hook. If there is a lesson to be learned or a new course of action to test, do it. Just do it without a cluttered mind. This is easier when you have recharged your batteries.

Recharge Your Batteries

Leadership can be exhausting. It is easy to get weighed down by the impact of the decisions you need to make. Because of this, leaders need to know how to recharge their batteries. This is different for all of us, but it is critical that we know what replenishes our energy and that we are wise enough to make time for it.

To get our battery semi-charged, we do need to focus on the basics. This includes things like getting good sleep, eating well, exercising, taking breaks. But if we want to fully replenish our batteries, especially as leaders making tough decisions, we need to do more. We need to pay attention to the things that have meaning, that bring us joy, that make us feel like we are making a difference. For many of the leaders we spoke with this includes reflecting on their role outside of work, focusing on the important relationships in their lives, and giving back to their communities.

A reflection exercise where you write your obituary can be a helpful way to confirm what is really important in your life. It can help you reflect on how you want to be seen and the legacy you would like to leave. The following are nine steps to guide you through the process:

1. Set aside an hour when you won't be interrupted. Turn off your devices and put them away.

2. Find a comfortable place to sit. Set a timer for ten minutes. Find a comfortable body position where you are relaxed and yet still alert.

3. Allow your attention to naturally follow the rhythm of your breath. Allow the breath to breathe itself. Do not try to control it. Just breathe. Let your attention rest on the experience of breathing.

4. After a few minutes, allow yourself to imagine what your funeral would be like. Imagine the people who would be there. The sorrow they would experience.

5. Now consider things that different people would say about you and about your life.

6. After a few minutes sitting with this experience, bring your attention back to the breath. Let go of any sadness that arose during the exercise. Let your attention rest on the experience of breathing until the timer ends.

7. Now, reflecting on this experience, consider what you would like people to think and say about you now and when you are gone. Consider your aspirations—what kind of person do you want to be?

8. Take time to write an obituary based on your aspirations for the life you want to live, which may be different from the life you are currently living.

9. Now make note of any changes that you want to make in your life right now that will help you steer more toward the life you want.

In our experience, one of the deterrents to doing the things that are most important to us and give us the most joy is a lack of time. It's true, time is limited. And none of us have time to do all the things we want to do. But time management is not about wishing you had more time. Instead, it's about making tough choices about how to use the precious time you do have. If something is truly important to you, make time for it.

Do It for You—Do It for Others

Imagine that you're on a plane and the captain comes on the intercom and says, "We have a problem with our mechanical system. We're losing cabin pressure. Please put on your oxygen mask."

Would you say, "Okay, but first I just need to finish typing this email"?

We are living in challenging and uncertain times. Our people are looking to us as leaders to have the wisdom and mental reserves to remain in the eye of the storm. To do this well, we need to prioritize taking care of ourselves. When we don't take care of ourselves, we're no good to ourselves or to our people.

It is not innate human aggression that sometimes makes us aggressive. It is more often our lack of care and respect for ourselves. There is an often-used axiom: Hurt people hurt people. This means that people who have been harmed have a greater tendency to do harm to others. When we are not caring for ourselves, we're not able to care for others. And when we don't fully respect ourselves, we will lack the full respect of others. The path to strong leadership is not to be self-critical of ourselves, but rather to care for ourselves and respect ourselves—so we can do the same to the people we lead. When you look at it this way, taking time for yourself can be seen as selflessly serving your people. It also allows you to be a good role model for your people so that they do the same.

Having our own oxygen mask on enables us to pause and take a breath, so that we can be more intentional as leaders. But in bringing more wisdom and compassion into our leadership, we need to understand that busyness can kill our heart.

5

Busyness Kills Your Heart

Why do people help in some situations, but not in others? This is an eternal question that social psychologists John Darley and Daniel Batson tackled in a famous experiment called the "Good Samaritan" study.[1] Their study involved sixty-seven seminary students, people who you would expect to always do the right thing. They asked all sixty-seven students to deliver a sermon on helping strangers in need. Darley and Batson then chose some students to be "hurried" and some to be "unhurried." The hurried students were told that they were running late to deliver their sermons. These students rushed off. The unhurried students were told they had time before they were due to deliver their sermons, but they might as well start walking over to the venue anyway. Each student, whether hurried or unhurried, headed alone to the building where they were supposed to deliver the sermon.

On the way, they ran into a man slumped in a doorway. His eyes were closed, and he was moaning and coughing. He was clearly in distress and needed help.

Would the students stop to help the stranger in need, Darley and Batson wondered? It was, quite literally, the topic of their sermons. As somewhat expected, over 60 percent of the unhurried students stopped to help the man. But surprisingly, only 10 percent of the hurried students stopped. To them, it was more important to be on time and keep to their schedules than to help a human being in distress.

As busy leaders, how often do we not stop and help people in need?

Too many of us rarely make time for what matters. In one of our surveys, we assessed over a thousand leaders, and 91 percent said that compassion is important or very important for leadership, but workload and other demands get in the way.

There is ancient Chinese wisdom in the word "busyness": it consists of two characters, one meaning "killing" and the other meaning "heart."

This idea that busyness kills your heart is not just figurative; it is also literal. Numerous studies show that task overload, mental stress, and busyness are associated with physiological hyperreactivity, including increased blood pressure and impaired connectivity between the heart-and-brain response.[2]

Take a moment to pause and reflect on your experience with busyness.

Would you describe yourself as busy?

Consider for a moment what that means for you.

Does it mean you are under a lot of pressure and have more tasks to do than time to do them? Does it mean you don't have time for other activities or people that are important?

If we are too busy to care, we are in trouble as leaders. But being "busy" is the prevailing state of leadership today. In this chapter, we explore our attachment to busyness, how it impacts our leadership, and how we can become more compassionate leaders by overcoming busyness.

What's So Great about Being Busy?

Consider this scenario: Imagine that you are catching up with a friend who is in a leadership position. You ask how she is doing, and she says, "Great! Things are really calm at work and everything is simple and easy and going well." Chances are, you would think she is either lying to you or about to get fired. In today's work context, being busy is equated with being important. If someone says they are not busy, we assume they are lying, lazy, or incompetent. Recent research even finds that busyness and lack of leisure time—showing that one isn't taking all their allotted holiday time—are used as status symbols.[3]

But should we really place so much value on busyness?

Let's have a closer look at what being busy actually means. From a neurological perspective, the experience of busyness activates our sympathetic nervous system. This system helps our body respond to potential threats in our environment by activating our fight-flight-freeze response. It can be thought of as putting our foot on the gas pedal in our bodies, activating a stress response that kicks us into action.

This drive for action can be very helpful. It enables us to get things done, to overcome procrastination, and in a number of situations it can enhance our performance. But a constant experience of being busy means our bodies are never at rest. We are "always on" and never taking the time to slow down. It can be detrimental to our health and our leadership.

Consider this scenario: Imagine that you are leading a critical meeting with your team. You have a packed agenda, and there are some key decisions you need to make today. To connect before you dive into the agenda, you decide to spare a few moments at the start of the meeting to invite everyone to check in. The first person's check-in takes too long. You can feel the stress response activated in your body, but you calmly suggest that in the interest of time everyone take just one minute each.

When you are more than three quarters of the way through your team, John shares that he is not doing well and is having a really bad day.

If the first thought that goes through your mind is "We don't have time for this!," don't worry. You are human, and you would not be the first or last leader who under pressure finds it difficult to lead with great wisdom or great compassion. Being busy is one of the main reasons that we end up in Quadrant 3 (Ineffective Indifference) of the Wise Compassion Matrix, as shown in figure 5-1.

FIGURE 5-1

Quadrant 3: Ineffective indifference

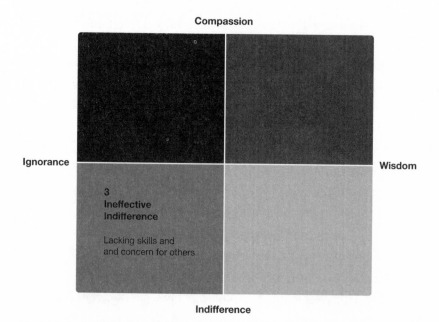

Now, we are not saying that you should forgo the entire agenda to find out why John is having a tough time. But note that if your default reaction to the suffering of one of your colleagues is "I don't have time for this," then, in that moment, you are squarely in Quadrant 3 and at risk of an ineffective and indifferent response.

And just to be clear, we can all end up in this quadrant—not because we are uncaring people, but because of busyness. When we feel we don't have enough time, when we feel under pressure, we are at risk of losing our compassion. When we are in this state of busyness, we are not as caring or attentive to people around us. We might miss cues that indicate that someone did not understand our comment or explanation. We are more prone to default to our habits and operate in ways based on biases. In essence, being busy means we are more likely to be at risk of being indifferent and in-effective as leaders.

The Attraction of Busyness

Before we turn to how best to manage this problem, it is helpful to understand why being busy can feel good even when we know it has negative consequences for our leadership and our health. Very simply put, we choose to stay busy because it makes us feel productive and because it is addictive.

Busyness Feels Productive

Busyness is seductive because we confuse an active mind with a productive mind.

When we have lots of ideas and thoughts pinging around our brain, we can be fooled by the illusion that we are keeping on top of things. Consider whether you can relate to the following question: "How can I keep my edge if my mind isn't racing at 100 miles per hour with a million thoughts?"

But is it really true that having "a million thoughts" results in greater productivity?

Consider the last time you had a really good idea. Was it when your mind was cluttered or when your mind was clear? More than likely, it was when you stopped thinking and created more space in your mind. This is why so many great ideas come to people while taking a shower, during a walk, or even while sleeping.

But this is not our default mode of operating. Our brain has a natural tendency to ruminate. If there is something we are concerned about, our brain will replay the same thoughts over and over again, trying to help us come up with an answer or learn a lesson.

This is when our brain can play a cruel trick on us. It can create the illusion of a "busy" mind being productive because we convince ourselves that by replaying the tape over and over again, at some point the issue will be resolved. But in fact, our mind is just stuck in a hamster wheel, and we are wasting precious mental energy. But because we are thinking about a problem we need to solve—because we're making a conscious effort—we can be tricked into thinking a busy mind is good. As most of us are painfully aware, however, rumination just leads to more rumination. And rarely, if ever, does it lead to insight or letting go. Busyness kills our compassion by cluttering our mind and closing ourselves to the wisdom and insight that comes when we have more mental space.

Busyness Is Addictive

Being busy is addictive—and by addictive, we mean physically addictive, like a nicotine or alcohol addiction.

It may sound overly dramatic, but it's true.

When we complete a task, even an insignificant task like sending an email, dopamine is released in the brain. Dopamine is a naturally produced and highly addictive hormone. When released in the brain, it provides a sense of enjoyment and gratification. Because of this feeling, our brains are constantly looking for another dopamine hit—and quick, easy tasks like answering email, responding to a text, or updating our calendars can give us a "fix." The problem is, dopamine does not distinguish between activity and productivity, between mere busyness and true efficiency. This makes us effective at doing a lot of things, but not necessarily at doing the important things.

In a *Harvard Business Review* article titled "Beware the Busy Manager," researchers shared findings on leaders' ability to prioritize tasks. Studying leaders in companies such as Sony, LG, and Lufthansa, the researchers concluded, "Very few managers use their time as effectively as they could. They think they're attending to pressing matters, but they're really just spinning their wheels."[4] Another study looked at the priorities of three hundred fifty thousand people and found that they spent an average of 41 percent of their time on low-level priorities. In other words, we're doing a lot of things—just not the right things.[5]

A recent study found that work-addicted managers can be a negative influence not just on themselves but for their employees, teams, and the broader organization. This shows that the impact of busyness pervades throughout the organization and creates a sort of ecosystem of always-on but never really getting important work done.[6]

The consequence of this addiction is that we're constantly chasing quick wins and easy fixes at the expense of long-term goals. When we do this, our ability to prioritize suffers, our willingness to do hard things deteriorates, and our overall performance diminishes. Remember, activity is *not* productivity. And the pleasure we get out of completing a task—any task, no matter how trivial—is just a temporary chemical reaction, much like a sugar high.

Fortunately, there are a number of steps we can take to overcome our busyness addiction.

We Can Overcome Busyness

If we want to enable our innate compassion to come to the surface, we need to overcome busyness. We need to let go of the value we place on being busy and find ways to be more disciplined and effective with our time. To do so, we need to recognize that busyness is a choice. Then we need to manage our time, make people a priority, and value busylessness. Let's take a closer look at each of these strategies.

Busyness Is a Choice

Our minds enjoy being busy. Many cultures value busyness and see it as a badge of honor. We all have a lot to do and not enough time. But fundamentally, whether we want to be busy or not is a choice. If we have ten things that we absolutely must get done today and we only have time to get six of them done, we can choose whether to experience busyness. We can choose to be overwhelmed and feel under pressure. Or we can make a wise mental choice to prioritize the six we will do and stop thinking about the four important things that we just don't have time to do today.

Time is finite. We all wish we had more hours in the day. But we don't. If we resist the urge to feel pressured by limited time, we can make more of the time we have by lifting our foot off the gas pedal and having a more calm, clear mind to do what we can get done.

Again, this is our choice.

The research on busyness and task productivity shows a clear link to an individual's perceptions; that is, it isn't actual busyness that drives these outcomes but instead perceived busyness—the person convincing themselves that everything around them is busy.[7] That it is merely a perception suggests that it is something that can be changed by simple framing techniques and self-regulation. There's also a clear link to people's confidence within themselves, such that people with poor self-efficacy (low confidence) tend to feel greater time pressure and to report being busier. They also feel more competitive in that state of busyness and as a result display reduced compassion and less motivation for helping others.[8]

As noted earlier in the chapter, stress activates our sympathetic nervous system, triggering our stress response. This increases our heart rate and shifts the flow of blood and oxygen away from our brain and toward our lower extremities, so we are ready to run or fight. As a leader facing hard decisions and wanting to do them in human ways, would you rather have blood and oxygen flowing toward your brain or away from it?

If we can take a moment to pause, realistically appraise what we can get done, *choose* not to be busy, and therefore not be stressed, we can activate our parasympathetic nervous system. When we activate our parasympathetic nervous system, it is like stepping on our internal brake pedal. It enables our body to slow down, relax, rest, and feel at ease. From this state of mind, we can better tackle the things we need to do because we are calmer and have much greater clarity.

Manage Time and Priorities

We worked with a senior leader who was well liked by his colleagues and team. But he had a habit of being unrealistic about when he could get something done. He would often say, "I will get back to you tonight," and every member of his team would know that was highly unlikely. He had the right intentions, and he was a smart guy. But good intentions and high IQ combined with lack of wisdom regarding time management equals poor outcomes.

Being able to realistically assess time and priorities is hard. It takes discipline, experience, and practice. This is wisdom in action. Overcoming busyness by better managing time and priorities enables us to be a wiser *and* more compassionate leader. This takes ruthless prioritization and disciplined assessment of time. Too many of us have a lot to do and hope somehow we can get it all done. But in the back of our minds, we know we can't, and so the foot is still on the gas pedal, creating excessive stress. The only way to take the foot off that pedal is if we take time to be ruthless in assessing our priorities and disciplined in evaluating and managing our time. This should be done quarterly, monthly, weekly, and daily so that we always have the big picture in mind to ensure we are getting the right things done.

Morten Hansen, author of *Great at Work* and coauthor of *Great by Choice*, has a simple expression for ruthless prioritization: "Focus isn't focus unless it hurts."[9] The wisdom in this is a recognition that we all have more things that we want to do than we have time for. Real focus requires painful choices about what is really important versus what is important, but we need to let go. Jony Ive, a former senior executive at Apple, shared his experience working with Steve Jobs. When he would go into his office to talk about priorities, Jobs would pressure him to declare what he was *not* going to do. Invariably, when he would offer his list, Jobs would say, "Not good enough—come up with something else."[10] For Jobs, focus was about making sacrifices and saying no to things that you really didn't want to let go of, but had to so that you could truly focus. The following are some tips to help you overcome busyness through better time management and the clarification of your priorities:

- Clear Mental Clutter: Take time to cultivate a sense of relaxation, release the pressure gauge, and create more clarity of mind. One of the best ways to do this is by practicing mindfulness. As we have discussed in our previous books, mindfulness training is a simple and powerful tool to activate the parasympathetic nervous system, enabling our mind and body to relax. When we need to make difficult decisions, especially about competitive priorities, it is always best to do this with a calm, clear mind.

- **Assess Priorities:** Take time to review what needs to be done. Assess what is important versus what is urgent. Assess how much time tasks or activities will realistically take. Review how much time you have. Make tough decisions about what you can and cannot do, and then be diligent about planning your time.

- **Manage Your Time:** Block off time in your calendar to ensure you give yourself the time you need to get things done. Be ruthless. Include buffer time for tasks that take longer than expected. Block off time for breaks to reactivate the parasympathetic nervous system. Block off time for unexpected issues, so that you have time for unplanned events and don't get stressed.

Depending on your time frame, these three steps can take anywhere from an hour to five to ten minutes. By being more disciplined with your time, you will find that you are able to get more of the right things done. You will also find that you may be able to get more things done. When your mind is clear, you are more efficient than when your mind is cluttered. You are a kinder, wiser leader. And you can be more creative about how to address issues and solve problems, especially those related to managing people.

Put People First

Leadership is about people. The role of leading is to take time to support and enable others to get things done. This should be where you spend most of your time. If you find that you are "too busy" to focus on supporting and developing others, you have a problem.

Take a moment to reflect on your to-do list. How many items on it are related to you doing things versus you enabling others to do things? If there are too many things in the first category, it may be an opportunity to rethink your priorities and your role as a leader.

Here are some tips that can help ensure that you "put people first" as a way to help overcome busyness:

- **Prioritize People in Your Calendar:** Take a moment to consider what percentage of time you think you should be devoting to supporting and developing others. Now look at your calendar for the next week. In particular, look at every meeting you are scheduled to attend. How many of these are devoted to supporting and developing others? Are there opportunities for you to cancel things to give more time for people?

- **Leverage Development Opportunities:** Are there some things you are doing that you could give to someone else as a development opportunity? And yes, this could mean that it might not be done as quickly or exactly as you would like, but if you take a longer-term view, challenge yourself to create more space for you and more opportunities for others. Long term, it's a win-win.

- **Create a To-Be List versus a To-Do List:** Consider what kind of leader you want to be. This could include things like how you want to show up for others, or how you want to inspire them or make them feel supported. Sometimes we forget that we are human "beings" as opposed to human "doings." To overcome busyness, it can be helpful to put the things we want "to be" as a leader at the center of our stage more often. Create your to-be list and post it prominently in your workspace so you remember to put people first.

Value Busylessness

Here is a radical idea. What if we placed more value on not being busy? What if we allowed ourselves to have more moments of non-doing and just being? Too many of us associate not doing anything with being unproductive or lazy. Since we are wired for activity and doing things, a natural discomfort often arises when we do nothing. Valuing busylessness is to invite and familiarize yourself with the experience of doing nothing. This experience is the mother of creativity and well-being. But before those arise, we must pass the threshold of discomfort of feeling like we are wasting our time.

Busylessness is productive inner silence. At first, it can feel of limited benefit. But after a while, we start to notice thoughts and emotions that we were not previously aware of. "If you just sit and observe, you will see how restless your mind is," Apple founder Steve Jobs told biographer Walter Isaacson. "If you try to calm it, it only makes things worse, but over time it does calm, and when it does, there's room to hear more subtle things—that's when your intuition starts to blossom and you start to see things more clearly and be in the present more. Your mind just slows down, and you experience tremendous expanse in the moment. You see so much more than you could see before. It's a discipline; you have to practice it."

Valuing nonaction can also be applied to how we lead others. Sometimes as leaders, in our desire to be compassionate we can be too quick to act. Sometimes, not taking action can be the wisest and most compassionate thing we can do to create space for people to figure things out on their own. This requires discipline.

For most of us, the easy thing to do when someone comes to us with a problem is to jump in and try to solve it. And although sometimes that can be helpful, valuing busylessness is about challenging ourselves to see what happens if we don't take any action at all.

Radical Acceptance

As we've said, hard things are hard. The more senior we are in an organization, the more difficult it will be to not feel pressure. The decisions that come to our desk are not easy ones. And we will need to constantly manage the pressure gauge in our body to keep the foot off the gas. Sandy Speicher, the CEO of the global design firm IDEO, spoke about the mental pressure of doing hard things, especially during uncertain times, as "feeling like compression in your mind. You are pushed to make fast decisions to alleviate the pressure." And taking quick action and being decisive can ease the pressure—but that is not always the best path forward. The compression on the mind can easily lead to the opposite of compassion because, as Sandy puts it, "It feels like there is no time for care—you just want to act." However, the ability to be in the situation, to endure the pressure, can lead to learning and insights that result in better decisions. For Sandy, this means "to design, not decide. To design is the ability to go on a journey to find the answers, rather than start with them." So, toughing it out, enduring the pressure, and staying in the ambiguity are important.

Staying in the ambiguity requires radical acceptance. Of course we will feel under pressure. Of course there are going to be moments or days when busyness kills our compassion. Cultivating radical acceptance is helpful in enabling us to be okay when things are not as we would like them to be and also when we are unable to be the kind of leader we would like to be.

Radical acceptance is accepting the things we really want to be different but cannot change. It requires sitting with the discomfort of things that are uncomfortable. It requires embracing our resistance to wanting things to be different.

Ultimately, overcoming busyness and enabling our compassionate nature to come to the forefront is about managing how our mind deals with hard things. If we allow our mind to get caught up in the pressure of hard things and become cluttered and pressured, we are at risk. If we are able to slow down and assess what is most important, we can avoid the trap of falling into Quadrant 3 and respond to hard situations with more wisdom and compassion.

To make this practical, let's revisit the team meeting scenario from earlier in the chapter. Although there is no guaranteed "right" answer—remember, hard things are hard—let's walk through what a potential "wise" and "compassionate" response could look like:

- **Take a Breath:** Let go of the "I don't have time for this" reactive response. Remember the research on the Good Samaritan. There is always time for caring for people. It doesn't have to take over the whole meeting, but you can take an unhurried moment to acknowledge what John is experiencing.

- **Express Care:** Thank John for sharing and show genuine concern. Consider this quote from Maya Angelou: "People won't remember what you said, but they will always remember how you made them feel." Say what comes naturally to you, tap into the compassionate area of your brain, and set an intention to make John feel seen and heard. After all, we have all had moments like this—you have too. Show you care.

- **Provide Options:** Consider possible ways forward that do not involve derailing the agenda but that acknowledge John's state of mind. Ideally, engage him in the process by giving him options on how to move forward. For example, you could ask, "Are you okay to participate in this meeting, or would it be better for you to take a break?" Or "Is there anything that we can do right now to support you, or are you okay if we continue with the agenda, and you and I can follow up later?"

In most situations, taking time to make someone feel valued saves time. Why? Because although it isn't guaranteed, showing you care could help make other people's days a little brighter, make them feel that they're not alone, make them feel more connected with the team, and enable them to more fully participate in meetings or other collaborative efforts. When we open our hearts to each other, we give ourselves more space to connect as compassionate beings. And this allows us to feel better about being part of a caring team that has more strength to face difficulties.

This is the power of wise compassion in action.

Clarity, People, and Presence

Too many of us waste mental time and energy ruminating about things we don't have time to do. But the truth is, there's never enough time in the day to get everything done and still have time for self-care or other life-nourishing activities. This is why it is so important to be clear about your most important priorities for the day. Once we're able to establish clear priorities, we can stop cluttering our minds with less important tasks that we realistically don't have time to achieve. When we allow our minds to be cluttered and busy, it is harder to see what is really most important in the moment. We're blind to what happens right in front of us, because we're too busy with everything that's bouncing around in our minds. In this way, our intellect can become our worst enemy in seeing clearly and doing what needs to be done—leading with wisdom.

In contrast, the ability to "let go" of things we cannot do enables us to be more focused and less stressed, allowing us to more effectively engage in the things we are doing. If we focus on what we can and should do in this moment, we can focus on the task at hand or the person we are with. This means we can make people feel seen and heard and show them respect by being in the moment. And by being in the moment, we can meet people where they are and open our arms to their suffering with wise and compassionate presence. In the next chapter, we look at the importance of presence and how to be sure you are working—and living—in the moment.

Be Here Now

When you are present, you are in the moment, giving the people around you your full attention. Only when you are fully present can you lead with wise compassion. In fact, in our research, we found that leaders who reported practicing mindfulness, which helps us to be present in everyday life, were rated as significantly wiser and more compassionate by their direct reports compared to leaders who practiced mindfulness less frequently or did not practice it at all. Figure 6-1 shows the relationship between mindfulness practice and wisdom and compassion.

The data clearly show that regular mindfulness practice makes leaders more present and thereby able to show up with greater wise compassionate leadership. Because of this, "caring presence," with the mantra "Be here now," is the foundation for wise compassion and the first step of the Wise Compassion Flywheel, as shown in figure 6-2.

To enter into difficult situations with others, we must start by being present and do it with care. When we are present, we can choose wise compassion as our approach, and we can make the choice to be here now. Leadership is about connection, and there is no possibility of connection if we are not present—if we aren't

FIGURE 6-1

Mindfulness practice enhances wisdom and compassion

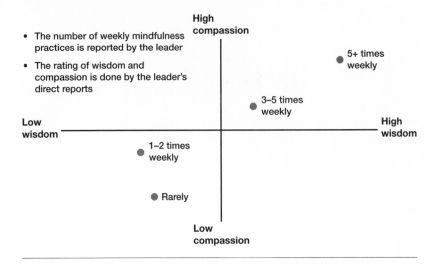

- The number of weekly mindfulness practices is reported by the leader
- The rating of wisdom and compassion is done by the leader's direct reports

there, we can't care. The reverse is also true. When we are fully present, we have a better chance of making a meaningful connection, and it is easier for us to bring wisdom and compassion to the table.

Steve Mizell, CHRO of Merck, told us that he believes one of the most critical skills for leaders today is to slow down and be more fully present with people, to really check in, and to listen more deeply. And this need becomes exacerbated when we do hard things. "As leaders we have great impact on the people we lead," Steve said. "And sometimes we have to do difficult things. In those situations, it is imperative that we are truly present and take the time to get vested in our people's current state of mind."

The importance of this cannot be overrated. A recent survey study found that when leaders are distracted by their phones, it undermines supervisory trust, which, in turn, lowers employee engagement.[1] Being present is important. Period. Hard things are hard. But hard things are impossible if we are not fully there.

FIGURE 6-2

The Wise Compassion Flywheel—caring presence

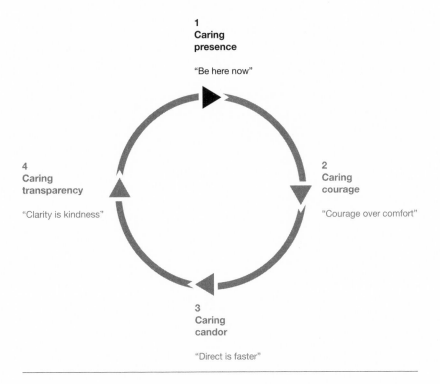

1
Caring
presence

"Be here now"

4
Caring
transparency

"Clarity is kindness"

2
Caring
courage

"Courage over comfort"

3
Caring
candor

"Direct is faster"

In fact, if you want to do "hard things" really poorly then be inattentive.

Amid challenges, however, it is difficult to be fully present. We are easily distracted. It can be hard to slow down when we have so much to do. And even when we are able to be "in the moment," we can get caught up with our own stories and projections about what is happening. We can be influenced by our biases or driven by our ego. So, although "being here now" sounds simple and is important, in practice, it is not so easy.

The challenges to being present are why sometimes we unintentionally end up in Quadrant 3 of the Compassionate Leadership Matrix and act in ways that are ineffective and indifferent. And although this seems like a place we would never want to be, all of us end up there from time to time—not because we are bad leaders, but because we are human. Being human means sometimes we aren't attentive either to ourselves or to others. But we are not stuck. When we pay attention to paying attention, we can bring more wisdom and compassion to our leadership through greater caring presence.

There are three aspects of caring presence that are critical for wise compassionate leadership. The first is being present with what is happening right now versus being distracted. The second is being present with yourself, knowing what is important to you, and recognizing any traps that might get in your way. The third is being present with others to tune in to what they are expressing but may or may not be saying.

Be Aware to Be Present

Despite good intentions, the reality is that many of us are too distracted to be fully present with other people. We want to be attentive; we might even think we are paying attention. But in reality, we are somewhere else.

In our research with thousands of leaders across the globe, we found that during working hours, we are distracted 37 percent of the time. The range on either side of this 37 percent average is driven up or down by several important factors. Looking at age, for example, we see that younger people in organizations are more distracted than older ones. People in their twenties and thirties tend to get distracted during the workday roughly 40 percent of the time, with their more senior counterparts and colleagues in their fifties and sixties being distracted about 30 percent of the time. This difference is paralleled by the seniority level of the leader in the organization: junior, entry-level associates report being distracted 42 percent of the time compared to high-ranking executives, who are distracted about 32 percent of the time. And finally, in relation to geographic region, our global sample reveals that leaders in Asia Pacific, South America, Africa, and the Middle East all fall within the 37 to 38 percent average estimate of distractedness, while North Americans fare the worst at 40 percent, and Europeans the best at 32 percent. Interestingly, top-performing countries include Austria (14 percent), Switzerland (25 percent), and Germany (27 percent).

In our previous books—*One Second Ahead* and *The Mind of the Leader*—we have written extensively about how we are wired for distraction and how we can train our minds to be more in the moment. We will not repeat all of the same background information and benefits here, but instead focus on some basic tenets of staying in the moment and provide specific strategies for being here now with others as the foundation for wise compassion.

We can all agree that wise leadership flourishes with a clear mind. When your mind is clear and sharp, you know instinctually, moment to moment, what is important to you and what is the right thing to do. When the mind is clear, it is like a sky without clouds distorting your view. Obsessive, ruminating thoughts that constantly clutter your thinking are like clouds, making your thought process slow and unclear.

These days, a clear mind is difficult to experience. We live lives tethered to streams of information through our devices, constantly notifying us of messages, calling for our attention with alerts, and making it difficult for the mind to just be. In fact, some of us might not even know what it means to have clarity of mind.

When we allow our minds to be cluttered and busy, it is harder to see what is most important in the moment. We are blind to what is happening right in front of us because we are too busy with everything that is going on inside our mind. We are prone to act on autopilot and default to ingrained behaviors. We are driven by our biases and are limited in our ability to see new ways of thinking or acting. We are also more prone to be driven by our ego.

To help you bring more wisdom and compassion into your leadership, being here now starts with mindful awareness. With more mindful awareness you can better understand yourself, your mind, and how you can maintain a higher level of caring presence.

Mindful Awareness

Leadership starts in the mind.

To rewire our minds, we have to start with being aware of what to rewire. Without awareness of what is happening in our minds, it's like being blindfolded. Mindful awareness helps us manage our attention by enabling us to be aware of what is happening within the landscape of our mind. It helps us to be more attentive to our external environment, as well as our internal processes, including what we are thinking and feeling. With greater mindful awareness we can be more intentional about where we choose to place our attention and what we choose to let go.

There are many ways we can enhance our awareness. One of the most simple and effective ways is through the practice and application of mindfulness. Learning to manage your attention is at the center of the practice of mindfulness. When you learn how to manage your attention, you learn how to manage your thoughts. You learn to hold your focus on what you choose, whether it's this page, an email, a meeting, or the people you are with. In other words, you train yourself to be more present in the here and now.

Because of neuroplasticity, our awareness can be enhanced. We can change the ratio of our conscious to unconsciousness behaviors, which can make the difference between making good or bad decisions. But what is awareness really? Do you know what awareness feels like? Follow these steps to take a moment to experience it:

1. Let go of this book. For one minute, sit still.

2. Whatever comes into your mind, be aware of it. Simply notice it.

3. Let go of any inner commentary of why you are doing this exercise.

4. No analyzing, no judging, no thinking.

5. Simply be aware.

6. Just be.

This is awareness: a direct experience of what is happening to you right now.

Mindful awareness is the starting point for becoming a wise leader. It helps you to clear mental clutter, understand more of the inner workings of your internal landscape, and be more objective in how you manage your mind. In this sense, mindful awareness is the foundation for any leadership journey. As part of this journey, it is helpful to understand that you and your thoughts are not the same thing.

You Are Not Your Thoughts

The more time you spend training your awareness, the more you'll come to fully appreciate that you are not your thoughts. Just because you have a bad thought doesn't make you a bad person. Your thoughts are not you.

Awareness training helps you create a healthy and realistic distance from your mental activities. You start to observe your thoughts as fleeting events that have no real substance or importance. They're just like those clouds in the sky mentioned earlier: they come and go. And they only have an impact on you if you allow them to. Yes, many of our thoughts and feelings spark emotions or actions. But in truth, many of them are random and insubstantial. We don't need to react to them. We can simply let them be.

Once we realize this, we can be more objective. Doing this creates incredible freedom to choose our thoughts, or not. And when we choose what to think and what not to think, we change our reality.

Consider a simple example: You are in your car on your way to an important meeting, and someone speeds in front of you and cuts you off. A natural tendency is to construct a reality where the person in the other car is a self-serving jerk. But suppose you pause and interject a new train of thought: *What if this person is on his way to the hospital with a sick child in the backseat?* Now you are open to a new, more compassionate reality.

In more complicated scenarios, we can use mindful awareness to help us recognize negative thought patterns associated with biases or past experiences that limit our judgment and result in poor decisions. For example, when we are giving feedback to someone from a different culture, we can be aware of thoughts that are based on stereotypes and choose to be more curious and open-minded. This in itself is a significant step toward better understanding the power of our egos to control our thoughts and reactions.

Understand Your Ego

Most of us do not like to think that we are egoistic. We would like to think of ourselves as being kind, generous, and thoughtful of others. And although we can be all those positive things, we have all experienced moments when we are unkind, selfish, and self-centered. But this does not make us bad people. It provides an opportunity for us to enhance awareness of how our brain works and provides opportunities to act in ways that are more in line with our values.

So, if we are not bad people, why do we sometimes behave in selfish ways? Generally speaking, we behave in selfish ways because of how our brains are wired, specifically because of what is called our Default Mode Network (DMN).

Recent research has found that when we are not actively engaging in intentional mental activity, the brain naturally slides into this Default Mode Network. This research has shown that when the DMN takes over, not only are we aimlessly daydreaming, but we are also getting increasingly worried and unhappy.[2] This is because the DMN is designed to solely think about ourselves. And when we are left to think about ourselves, we start thinking about all of the things we need to do. Or things we wish we would have said or done. Or the things we are afraid we won't get done. Or the things we are afraid people will do to us or say about us. You get the idea. Research shows that on average, we spend 47 percent of our waking hours in this wandering mental mode.[3] This, in turn, means that for almost half of our waking hours we are susceptible to being unproductive and anxious—and certainly not the best leader.

In addition, when the DMN is activated, we see the world only from our own perspective. We don't put ourselves in the shoes of others and don't consider their perspectives.[4] In this way, the DMN is where our egos reside. By constantly ruminating on ourselves, it slowly creates a stronger false sense of identity, including a limited view of our ultimate potential.

In striving to lead with wise compassion, this is a problem. When we operate from the DMN, we are applying neither wisdom nor compassion. Even though this is our default mode of thinking, studies have shown that when we train in mindfulness and improve our sense of awareness, we lessen its impact.[5] Through mindfulness training, we can gradually rewire our brains to be less self-oriented and more selfless.

In our book *The Mind of the Leader*, we explore the benefits of selfless leadership and how to cultivate it for yourself, your team, and your organization. We will not repeat that content here, but reiterate the benefits of training the mind to become more "other-orientated" as a means of overcoming the downsides of ego. When you are caught up in your own ego, you cannot be wise. Instead, you are doomed to see things from your limited, self-referential point of view. And when you see everything through the lens of how it impacts you, it can be very difficult to control how you react or respond to difficult situations.

Your Reaction Is a Choice

Mindfulness—and increased awareness—permit us to create a space between stimulus and response. As leaders, and as human beings, we are constantly inundated with data. In every fraction of a nanosecond, our brain is assessing what to pay attention to and whether to react or not. And although many of our autopilot reactions are beneficial, like jumping out of the way of a bus, some are not so helpful, such as yelling at an employee for asking a "dumb" question.

"Between stimulus and response there is a space. In that space, it is within our power to choose our response. In our response lies our growth and freedom," wrote Victor Frankl, a World War II concentration camp survivor.[6] He is right, of course. We all have a degree of freedom, and it lies in that fraction of a moment, that millisecond, in which we choose a response. When we are under pressure and have a lot on our mind, however, that moment of freedom becomes even shorter, making us more reactive.

In his book *Thinking Fast and Slow*, Daniel Kahneman explains the two systems that drive the way we think.[7] System 1 is fast, intuitive, and emotional; System 2 is slower, more deliberative, and more logical. Although both modes are important, without mindful presence we can be easily driven by our faster, more emotional brain, which can create challenges for us as leaders.

Neurologically, when we train in mindfulness, we are trigger-ing a shift in cognitive control to our frontal brain regions—Kahneman's System 2. Through repeated practice, this enables us to perceive our world, our emotions, and other people without fight-or-flight, knee-jerk reactions and have better emotional resil-ience.[8] This change in neurological wiring helps us perceive situ-ations and make decisions more from our conscious mind, avoiding some emotional traps and our unconscious biases. Operating more from our prefrontal cortex also enhances our executive function, the control center for our thoughts, words, and actions.[9] A well-developed executive function allows us to better lead ourselves and others toward shared goals. With stronger prefrontal activity, we deactivate our tendency to be distracted, and we become more present, focused, and attentive.

The first step toward gaining this type of cognitive control, though, is to be aware that your reaction to any comment or event is a choice. With this awareness, you can begin to better utilize this space, this moment of growth and freedom, to respond with greater wisdom and compassion.

Mindful Presence with Others

So now we are committed to being mindfully aware. We are armed with an increased understanding of our thoughts, our egos, and our response options. We should be set, right? Well, not quite. Being present with others means that we need to tune into what they are experiencing. Despite our best intentions—and even with an increased sense of self-awareness—this is not easy. But mind-fulness practice helps.

Our data shows that when leaders practice mindfulness they ex-perience less stress and more connection with others. Mindfulness practice makes leaders be more in tune with their direct reports.

Mindful leaders more frequently experienced a sense of shared and mutual understanding of the world with their direct reports.

Furthermore, leaders' frequent mindfulness practice had a tangible impact on their direct reports, who experienced lower burnout and higher job satisfaction, job engagement, and organizational commitment, as well as improved job performance. Our results also suggest that the impact of leaders' mindfulness on followers' outcomes is channeled through wise compassion. In other words, leaders who practice mindfulness become wiser and more compassionate, and that in turn means that their direct reports are doing better.

In many ways, mindfulness practice is a means for unlocking other positive leadership behaviors. But even if you don't practice mindfulness, there are strategies that can help enhance your ability to be more present with others: it's not about you, be curious and don't make assumptions, let go of expectations, and use the power of the pause.

It's Not about You

When engaging in hard things, it is easy to focus on yourself. When you are about to have a tough conversation, you focus on what you will say and how you will respond to objections. It is also natural to feel nervous and anxious about the upcoming discussion. Ken Cooper, CHRO of Bloomberg, had a very clear message for other leaders struggling with the challenges of having to do hard things: "It's not about you. It's about them. They are the ones who will have a hard time receiving this message. Don't feel sorry for yourself. Don't make it easy for yourself. They are the ones who will suffer."

If you can remember it's about them, not about you, you can let go of your inner voice and be more present with what they are saying or not saying. If you aren't sure what we mean by "inner voice," it is the narrator in your head we discussed in chapter 4 that says things like "I am not sure how I am going to do this" or "I hope she doesn't get mad at me." We all have this inner voice, and when we engage in hard things, it can become incredibly verbose.

When engaged in a difficult conversation, this voice can have useful insights, but beware of rumination that can feel helpful but is just mental clutter. When you are in a conversation, when you want to be present with others, when you want to hear what others are saying, it is best to kindly ask this inner voice to be quiet. Practicing mindful awareness can help you recognize your inner voice and keep it quiet.

Be Curious and Don't Make Assumptions

We have all been on the receiving end of hard messages. We all know how we feel when we hear things we don't want to hear. And although it can be very useful to put ourselves in others' shoes, it can be a trap. Too often we think we know how someone feels and are blind to what they are actually experiencing. This makes it difficult to connect. It also makes the other person feel even worse, because they feel unheard, unseen, or simply misunderstood. Instead, to be more present with others, we need to set aside our biases, our assumptions, and our fears, and bring genuine curiosity to the conversation.

Curiosity starts with a beginner's mind. Try to see the situation and the person with fresh eyes instead of assuming that you know what they will say or how they will feel. In "hard" conversations, it is particularly important to pay attention to what they are saying, as well as what they are not saying. Be sure to notice their tone of voice, their body language, their facial expression. Is there anything you can sense that they may not be sharing? And instead of making assumptions about what you notice, ask questions.

Potentially insensitive questions start with assumptions like "I know this is really difficult for you" or "I understand how you feel" or "I know you are upset." These things could be true, but they are all assumptions based on our own experiences and biases. They fail to give space to the other person to have their own unique experience. And thus, they don't serve us well.

Wiser questions come from a place of genuine care and compassion. These questions could go something like "Would it be helpful for you to tell me how you feel?" Or "Is there anything I can do for you right now?" Or "Is there anything I can share or explain to help make this easier for you?"

Pamela Maynard, CEO of Avanade, shared with us how she strives to create space for people to be heard. She is intentional about seeking out the people in the room who might be holding back or might not feel comfortable speaking up and inviting them into the discussion. For Pamela, being attentive to the diversity of the group and creating space for diverse voices is key to creating a more wise, compassionate, and inclusive culture.

Let Go of Expectations

As leaders, we put time and effort into planning how we will engage in hard things like difficult conversations. In doing so, we naturally create expectations of how we hope the conversation will go. Although it is important to consider the impact of messages, if we want to be fully present with others, we need to let go of these types of expectations. Letting go of expectations does not mean that we don't consider potential scenarios. Planning for various outcomes is just good preparation. Letting go of expectations means that when we are in the moment we let go of what we hoped would happen, and that we are present with what is actually happening. Then we can adjust accordingly.

Letting go of expectations also means letting go of hopes that the person will see or acknowledge you as a wise and compassionate leader. Remember, it is not about you. And regardless of how well you prepare for and navigate the situation, you should let go of any expectations of recognition for your efforts.

It is also important to be able to let go of things the other person says in the moment. Remember, they are human. This is not easy for them. They may be upset. They may say things to you and about you that are not nice. Give space for this. You don't need to agree, but you can let them have a moment to express sorrow, frustration, anger, or shame. If you can let go of your own reactivity to any negativity, if you can pause and choose how you would like to react, you can create a space for them to be human.

Use the Power of the Pause

When we are engaging in hard tasks, it is easy for us to get caught up in the moment. Even if we say all the right things, we cannot control how other people will respond. And because these things are hard, chances are they may not react in the way that we hope or expect. This is why we need to be prepared with the "Power of the Pause."

The Power of the Pause is simple. The first step is to be aware of when and how we become triggered. Take a moment to consider your emotional hot buttons—situations in which you know you tend to react instead of responding. For example, when someone breaks down in tears, are you at risk of empathetic hijack, as discussed in chapter 3? Or when someone turns a situation around and blames you, are you at risk of getting angry, losing your compassion, and just focusing on getting the job done? Knowing your triggers in advance can help you remain more in the moment and in the space of wise compassion.

The second step is simply to stop. Take a moment to collect your thoughts. Take a breath. Notice the urge to react and take a few more breaths. Notice any unhelpful emotions, such as anger, frustration, or shame, arising. Be present with what you are experiencing, and see if by focusing on breathing, you are able to calm down and clear your mind.

The third step is to choose how you want to respond. If you are able to respond from a place of wise compassion, great. If you are wise enough to recognize that you may still be at risk of reactivity versus responsivity, a good option might be to pause the conversation and suggest following up at another time. The pause button is good to keep close at hand when doing hard things. It gives you space to choose your response and tap into your inner wisdom.

Presence Takes Courage

All of us have had moments when we are physically present but mentally somewhere else. It's natural. But it is also frustrating and can hamper engagement, connection, and productivity, both for you as a leader and for the people you manage. The starting point for engagement is caring presence. If you are not fully present with your colleagues, there is no chance for connection. And if you are not present in the moment, you literally cannot care. The most effective way you can create better connections and improve engagement with your people is to be more present. And by being more present, especially in a caring way, you can be more responsive, less reactive, wiser, and more compassionate in your decisions and actions.

Just think back to times in your own life when you have felt the gift of someone's undivided attention—when you felt seen and heard. Regardless of the circumstances, you likely felt valued and respected. These types of moments represent wise compassion in action. When we remember it is not about us, it is easier to open up and be more present with the person in front of us—the person who deserves our respect, our attention, our care, and our curiosity. As Jesper Brodin, the CEO of Ingka Group, IKEA, told us,

"I have learned that the most important thing is to show up. When doing hard things, you can't hide. You must show up and be present with those who are impacted by your actions."

Showing up and being present, instead of hiding, requires courage. In the next chapter, we look at how to develop a caring form of courage that drives the next step in the Wise Compassion Flywheel.

7

Courage over Comfort

Pamela Maynard—CEO of Avanade, a forty-five-thousand-person global technology company focused on digital innovation—shared a story with us about one of the hardest things she had to do as a leader. The role of CEO is a balance of priorities—it's important to inspire your workforce, drive business growth, manage stakeholders, and more. And in 2020, just six months into her role as CEO of Avanade, the organization and the world suddenly faced a global pandemic, and those priorities were put to the test. "It was an immensely challenging time for everyone, and it quickly became clear that the pandemic would have a massive impact on both our people and our business."

With the world locking down, there was a lot of economic anxiety. Many organizations had to make the tough call to reduce their workforce to keep their business afloat. But early on, Pam committed to protecting jobs, even as that felt like a risk:

> As a new CEO, it felt challenging to make this decision because I wanted to come in as a leader, drive growth, and hit my targets. But in this truly once-in-a-lifetime situation we found ourselves in, my most important responsibility was to take care of our people. There was no other option

and no greater priority. In those early days, it was not business as usual. Every moment, my job as a leader centered around helping people at Avanade feel safe and cared for—whether that was through reassurance that they would be supported if they had to step away to handle their new and unexpected responsibilities, access to mental health resources, or flexibility in their day-to-day routines.

Pam removed chargeability requirements for consultants in the early months of the pandemic and lifted PTO limits as people needed to step away. As a leader, she saw an opportunity to demonstrate real courage to steer the ship through difficult times. She shared a principle that has guided her throughout her career: "Feel the fear and do it anyway." In this moment, she felt the fear: the fear of not wanting to impact company performance or disappoint her stakeholders. In her experience, fear is a great teacher. It helps you reflect on what is important to you and seek your own inner wisdom. Overcoming her fear, Pam was able to navigate a truly unprecedented situation and demonstrate Avanade's values and purpose—to make a genuine human impact—with not just words, but action.

For Pam, the courage to overcome fear has been foundational in helping her learn, grow, and develop throughout her career. "As a leader you are in a position of power with people looking to you for guidance and direction. Sometimes you make mistakes, sometimes you have to make decisions that negatively impact people, sometimes you have to let people go for no fault of their own . . . it can be tough." But, as Pam acknowledged, when we have the courage to face the discomfort and do what needs to be done, we come out stronger and wiser. As she told us, "Leadership requires a caring courage that helps ensure you make wise decisions."

This is the role of leaders: to make and execute hard decisions. Therefore, making hard decisions often means that others will get hurt or disagree with you, resulting in a confrontation. Having the courage to willingly approach confrontations is one of the most important skills of wise compassionate leaders. When this skill is lacking, bigger problems are sure to arise over time. In our interviews, this was a recurring theme. Because of our neurological wiring for empathy, it is easier for us to smile and agree with others than to openly disagree and cause a confrontation. As a result, many companies are hampered by a "culture of niceness" that unintentionally leads people to not raise dissenting points of view. Although on the outside this may seem great—*look, everybody is friendly and happy!*—it's not. Instead, this type of purposeful or forced agreeability inhibits innovation, inhibits psychological safety, and hurts overall performance.

To be a wise compassionate leader, you must learn to be courageous—and learn it well. Otherwise, you are not being kind to others. And, maybe surprisingly, you cannot deliver your desired results. In this chapter, we explore the idea of caring courage—the second step in the Wise Compassion Flywheel as depicted in figure 7-1.

We start by examining courage over comfort and the fear-based boundaries we need to cross to bring more courage into our leadership. We then look at the importance of having the courage to be vulnerable and look into the dark corners of our own mind. Finally, we explore how to engage in courageous conversations and create more courageous cultures.

Courage versus Comfort

We are all comfort seekers. Yes, we like to challenge ourselves and enjoy experiencing something new, but in reality, our brain is wired to seek comfort—to take the easy path and not rock the boat—because it is safer.

FIGURE 7-1

The Wise Compassion Flywheel—caring courage

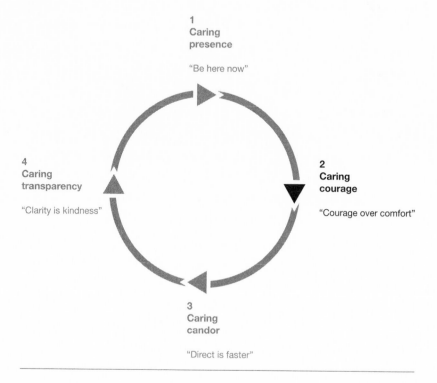

Overcoming our comfort-seeking orientation requires courage. Courage is different from fearlessness. With courage, we still experience fear or dread or concern. But courage is the inner strength to overcome our fear so we can take needed action or engage in a necessary confrontation. In this sense, courage is the willingness to move out of our comfort zones. For many people, it may seem counterintuitive, but our comfort zones can be dangerous. Yes, living in a comfort zone brings us a sense of security and certainty. It makes us feel safe. And, as human beings, we're hardwired to embrace this sense of certainty and safety. In fact, sometimes we'll do nearly everything we can to convince ourselves that staying in our comfort zone is the best thing for us.

In her book *Danger in the Comfort Zone*, Judith Bardwick describes the comfort zone as a psychological and behavioral state in which things feel familiar to us, along with the perception that we are in greater control of our environment. But as Bardwick outlines in her book, in our attempt to search out safety and comfort we may make decisions that are shortsighted and egocentric.[1] The pull to stay in our comfort zones limits our leadership potential because we avoid doing hard things and miss opportunities for growth and development.

If we want to be wise compassionate leaders, we need to develop and manifest courage. Wise compassionate leaders do not hide. They do not point their fingers at others and shirk responsibility. They do not avoid the hard things or difficult decisions. Wise compassionate leaders speak up when necessary and live their values. It is easy to stay in our comfort zone. But it is only when we get out of the comfort zone and find the courage to do hard things and face inevitable confrontations that we can be truly effective leaders.

It's important to remember that it is okay to seek comfort from time to time—we are human, after all. But we must understand and acknowledge the two different mindsets, so that we don't make decisions or lead from the comfort-seeking mind. In this way, courage is a personal choice. To help navigate choosing courage, it is helpful to explore some of the fears we need to overcome to bring more wisdom and compassion to our leadership.

Understanding Our Fears

To be a wise and compassionate leader, there are two primary fears we need to overcome: the fear of hurting others and the fear of hurting ourselves. We can examine these further using the Wise Compassion Matrix, as shown in figure 7-2.

To get out of Quadrant 1 (Caring Avoidance), we need to overcome our fear of hurting others. Because we are intrinsically good

FIGURE 7-2

The Wise Compassion Matrix

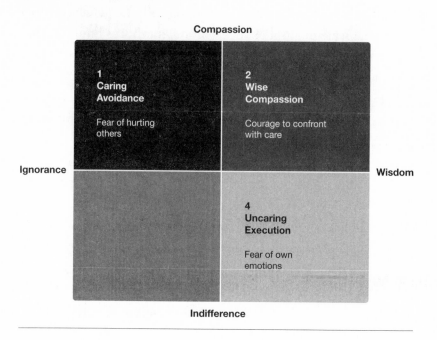

and want to be good to others, we're challenged as leaders because we sometimes have to inflict pain on others. This is uncomfortable for us and can make us refrain from doing what needs to be done. Wise leadership starts with learning to find the courage to enter uncomfortable situations with other people—and to stay in those situations, as uncomfortable as they may be. To be wise leaders, we must learn to find comfort in the discomfort of challenging situations in which we are inflicting some form of pain or difficulty on others. For many of us, when faced with the prospect of hurting another person we delay or avoid and end up being a "caring avoider" who leads from Quadrant 1.

But fear of hurting others is not the only fear we need to address in doing hard things to others. We also need to overcome the fears the underlie Quadrant 4 (Uncaring Execution) and face the fear of hurting ourselves. We don't like to think of ourselves as bad people. We don't like the idea that people will see us as being cruel or unkind. Therefore, our ego will protect us by putting up a shield that shuts off our emotions or tells us it's okay to be cold-hearted—that's part of the role as discussed in chapter 1.

This makes us robotic in dealing with hard things because we don't *dare to care.*

We don't want to feel the pain of feeling someone else's pain. This is not about them, it's about us. We close ourselves off to our own difficult emotions, which is easier on us. When we dull our own difficult emotions, we are losing touch with that very important side of being human and the opportunity it provides for human connection. In recognizing and giving space to our own suffering, we become familiar and comfortable with the foundational human condition of experiencing challenges. We find peace in discomfort. And in finding peace in discomfort, we radically strengthen our spiritual and psychological core. We gain a great confidence in our ability to weather storms and stand strong despite difficulties.

In addition to overcoming fears of hurting others or hurting ourselves, to be a wiser and more compassionate leader we must have the courage to dig deeply into our own limitations.

Understanding Ourselves

Wise compassionate leadership is to have respectful and caring confrontations with others. We can only master this when we are caring and respectful of ourselves, when we have self-compassion and self-confidence. Rewiring yourself for wise compassionate leadership is an inner journey of getting to know yourself, knowing what you stand for and what is important to you, and learning to manage your own inner limitations.

Take a moment to consider why you have chosen to be a leader.

More than likely, it isn't because you like being in charge and telling people what to do. You wouldn't be reading a book on compassionate leadership if you didn't have a heartfelt desire to support the development and success of others. Remembering your "why" can be helpful to boost your courage when the "what" and the "how" of leadership are challenging.

Further, it is important to do the work of knowing our inner enemies. These are the not-so-wise-and-compassionate parts of ourselves that hold us back from being the leader we want to be. They can come in many forms, including pride, shame, attachment, and ignorance. When we manage to find peace with our inner enemies, they no longer derail us from entering into confrontational situations with courage, respect, and care.

In our journey of getting to know ourselves, we will meet parts of ourselves that we are not proud of or that we wish were not there. Usually, we pay these versions of ourselves little attention and instead leave them conveniently buried. It's easier this way. But a main component of courage is our ability to become comfortable in confronting these aspects of ourselves—and even find peace with the fact that these negative traits are within all of us. This can be a painful process. Accepting that we are not as perfect as we would like to be is difficult. But the more we accept who we truly are, the more confidence we have simply because we have nothing to hide. Facing our imperfections is part of the path to finding our true power as leaders. It allows us to experience ourselves in a new way—it wakes us up to a higher level of self-awareness and acceptance.

In addition, as we start to see and accept our own imperfections, we become more tolerant and forgiving of other people's imperfections. We can see other perspectives and more easily connect with people by being vulnerable.

The Courage to Be Vulnerable

Vulnerability is often seen as a weakness. No one likes to expose their flaws. But when we have the courage to be vulnerable, we open a door to truly human connection. As leaders, we don't have all the answers. We don't always know the right thing to do, and we make mistakes. When we are vulnerable, we allow people to see our humility and our humanity. It also creates opportunities for them to be vulnerable, too.

Brené Brown, professor and author of *Dare to Lead*, states that "vulnerability is the last thing I want you to see in me, but the first thing I look for in you."[2] When we dare to be vulnerable about our challenges and emotions, the people we work with will see us more as a fellow human and less as a person higher on the organizational chart. From here we can cultivate a greater sense of humanness in our teams, which allows everyone to show up as whole human beings and bring more of their diverse skills and qualities. In showing yourself to be vulnerable about your challenges, you will spark the empathy of your team members and naturally let a culture of compassion arise. As Brown puts it, "In order for connection to happen, we have to allow ourselves to be seen."[3]

Stephanie Lundquist, former CHRO and executive vice president at Target, realized the importance of being vulnerable in the middle of the global pandemic. During lockdown there was so much going on for everyone. There was anxiety. There was stress. And Stephanie, like so many leaders, was checking in often with her direct reports on how they were feeling. But as she told us, "It wasn't until I shared with my team that I was struggling with my own resilience that I learned new things about what was really going on." For her, it was a vivid reminder of the power of vulnerability and how it unlocks the ability and willingness of others to share. Afterward, the team "shared so much more and became so much stronger because I demonstrated vulnerability."

In recognizing and embracing your own difficult emotions, you also become more attuned to the suffering and challenges of your team members. You become more aware of others' emotions if you are more aware of your own. In Daniel Goleman's extensive work on emotional intelligence, he has found that people with high emotional intelligence have greater awareness of both their own emotions and the emotions of others.[4] The opposite is also true: the more you dull your own emotions, the less sensitive you will be to how others feel. Therefore, recognizing and embracing your own emotions is critical to developing compassionate leadership. Learning to be with and embrace your own difficult emotions also helps you create a more compassionate and psychologically safe culture within your team.

Having confidence in who we are and embracing our limitations allow us to be more vulnerable, which creates the potential for wise and compassionate interactions. Tim Munden, chief learning officer at Unilever, shared with us that "compassion is not something you can do from a distance. You've got to be vulnerable." For him, a key element of compassion is about "having the courage to be totally open about myself—it's quite hard, to be compassionate if you're guarded." In his experience, he found that as he has become more vulnerable, more open, and more authentic, "compassion naturally flows." When we are more open with ourselves, it gives us the space to have the challenging conversations that we previously avoided.

Courageous Confrontations

Very simply put: If you cannot readily face conflict, you hinder your performance, negatively impact your career progress, and negatively impact the performance of your team or organization. Throughout his career, Jesper Brodin, CEO of Ingka Group, IKEA, has learned this lesson again and again. As he told us, "Through my career I have become more courageous. I had to. I have found that when I have been dishonest, it is because I wanted to protect the person in front of me. This, however, always turns out to be a disservice. And it slows down the organization. Real honesty is a compassionate thing. Compassion equals speed." The ability to enter into confrontational conversations without hesitation is a skill that Jesper developed through years of experience. We heard the same thing from other executives we talked to. They all agreed that a significant part of successful leadership hinges on the ability to get comfortable with being uncomfortable. Developing this type of inner strength requires that we learn to manage the discomfort of confrontations.

"Confrontation" is an emotionally loaded word for many of us. But it doesn't need to be. The essence of a confrontation is the friction, no matter how slight, between two or more parties, based on opposing views. Confrontations can be anything from a subtle disagreement—like whether or not we should mandate participation in all-hands meetings—to addressing issues of perceived discrimination, bullying, or harassment.

And here's our point: confrontations are positive.

If well managed, they are vital to increasing understanding, enhancing innovation, and implementing cultural change. To better develop wise compassionate leadership, it is important to recognize the fact that confrontations in themselves are not inherently negative. They only become negative when handled in unskillful ways—or when not handled at all. Confrontations, at their core, are merely expressions of two diverse points of views. When we enter confrontations with courage and an open mind, we can learn and grow. In this way, confrontation *should* be seen as an opportunity. Opposing views create new thinking, which leads to progress.

If we are driven by fear of the discomfort of the confrontation, we not only may lose the opportunity for development, we may also escalate the confrontation, creating a full-blown conflict. When leaders lack the courage to enter into candid and courageous conversations, everyone suffers. Brené Brown has found that this lack of courage diminishes trust and engagement, increases problematic behavior (including passive-aggressive behavior), increases negative gossip, and, due to a lack of clarity and shared purpose, decreases performance.[5] A lack of courage also lowers performance expectations for a team or an organization. If it is okay for one employee to perform at 80 percent capacity, then it becomes okay for everyone to perform at a lower level. Overall, when we are not confronting an issue with courage, it has negative impacts on people, teams, and culture.

Leena Nair, CHRO at Unilever, learned early on in her career the benefits of courageous confrontations for the benefit of the company. She once had a boss whose behavior often left her feeling humiliated and terrified. One day, she told her husband she had had enough and that she wanted to quit. He asked whether she had ever told her boss how she felt. "Are you kidding me?" she responded. "I can't stand in his office without getting scared. No, I'm not going to tell him anything." But upon reflection, she realized it wasn't just her who was suffering: the workplace was toxic, and the business wasn't growing. This gave her the courage to write him a letter detailing his negative behavior and the impact it was having on the team. To her surprise, his response was shock. He had no idea the impact he was having on the team. He asked for her help in changing his behavior, and they went on to have a great relationship.

Although not all stories of courageous confrontations have these kinds of happy endings, when we stand up for what we know is right, we are doing a service to ourselves and the organization. This is true regardless of our position in the organization and whether we are being courageous with a team member, a colleague, or, in Leena's case, the boss. Having courage over comfort when it is done for the right reasons is always beneficial. And bringing courage to the table is something that comes easier the more we get comfortable with the discomfort of confrontations.

Learn to Accept the Discomfort of Confrontation

Developing courage starts with getting to know yourself. The better you know yourself, the more you can step courageously into engagement—and even challenging conversations—with other people. Charlie Johnston, chief people officer at Mambu, had a true turning point early in his career. He was appointed the leader of two merged teams that traditionally were rivals. For months, Charlie avoided confronting the issue. But he knew in his gut that he had to make difficult changes. He also knew he needed to overcome his tendency to put difficult things off.

Only after a very heated team meeting that ended in a sleepless night did he decide to put an end to the conflict. As he shared with us, "I realized the problem started and ended with me. Only by stepping up with courage would I be of service to my entire team. On that day, I passed through a threshold of becoming a more courageous leader." This experience helped shape his leadership style and accelerate his rise through the company.

Courage is something we can all learn. And we learn it through doing it. First, like Charlie, we have to step through the threshold and let go of our fear. Then we simply must repeat it many times. Great courage comes from small acts of courage repeated many times through the years.

Research shows that when it comes to difficult emotions, avoidance and suppression techniques tend to make matters worse.[6] It is only when we intentionally face our fears that we can overcome the discomfort and over time expand our comfort zone to include things that before made us uncomfortable.

Developing your ability to manage confrontations with wisdom, care, and respect is not just a professional capability that will make you a better leader. It will also allow you to have more positive and constructive confrontations in your personal life. Wise compassionate confrontations offer a great journey of personal growth and liberation.

Strategies for Developing Courage

To rewire yourself for this type of leadership, you must first learn to manage your fear and turn it into courage. To find courage, start by asking yourself about your intention. Considering your intention can help you enter and stay in uncomfortable situations with others. If you know that your intention is positive, that you are intending to bring benefit to the person, it will ease the burden of the situation. As Ulrika Biesert, CHRO of IKEA, told us, "When I'm looking at myself in the mirror, I know that what I'm doing is best for the company and our people. But to know this, I need to be in full contact with myself. If I'm not, I can't be compassionate and I'm not utilizing my competence." The following are six strategies for developing courage.

- Strategy 1: Have at least one courageous confrontation every day. Make it a habit to have at least one courageous situation every day. It can be as small as giving a kind piece of feedback. The key is that it requires a little bit of courage from you. You will know that is does if it feels slightly uncomfortable.

- Strategy 2: Explore the impact of your courageous confrontations. Follow up on your courageous conversations. An hour or a day or a week later, ask people how they felt about your conversation. Explore whether it was helpful for them or not. Listen carefully and learn from what they experienced. By seeing that people are appreciating—or at least learning from—your courage and candor, this type of exploration can diffuse your fear of confrontations.

- **Strategy 3: Deal with things—never let them fester.** If you know something must be changed, do it. Don't let it fester. Don't leave people in suspense. They know something is not right, even if it hasn't been discussed. Nothing is as toxic as unacknowledged conflicts. So lead. Make decisions. Take action. Move forward.

- **Strategy 4: Trust your intuition.** If you feel that something is wrong, something likely is wrong. Trust yourself. Your entire system can detect difficult situations that need attention. Push beyond the fearful part of yourself that says everything will be okay if you pretend things are okay. You have a problem. Acknowledge it and move forward. It will only get worse the longer you wait.

- **Strategy 5: Get peer support.** When you find an issue particularly hard to confront, share it with a trusted peer. Be honest about the fact that you find it difficult. They may have a good or helpful idea. More likely, though, simply sharing your difficulty will help you. The fear that often holds us back increases when we keep it to ourselves, when we try to ignore it or bury it. When we share it with others, fear diminishes, and a sense of relief makes action more possible. Sharing with others and getting their input will also help you broaden your perspective and make you more effective in dealing with the situation constructively.

- **Strategy 6: Find the courage to endure.** One of the most challenging things for leaders to do is lead change. It requires courage to face resistance when others are out of their comfort zone. In 2016, Cris Wilbur, chief people officer at Roche, had a vision for how the human resources function could become more agile. Despite tremendous efforts, she and her team faced many organizational barriers. But fast forward two years later and people were coming to her asking why they weren't moving forward. As Cris learned, being courageous requires stamina and patience. It requires an understanding that just because you are able to make the leap, it may not be so easy for others to follow. In this way, wise compassion is about knowing when to push forward and having the courage to endure the discomfort of creating time and space for others to come onboard.

Courageous Cultures

If you create a culture of courage, you do not need to be the only courageous one in your company or on your team. Instead, it becomes a cultural expectation for everyone to be courageous. If everybody in the company embraces this purpose and if you have a common set of values, then it creates a cultural pressure to have the courage needed to speak up and do things in line with what is in the best interest of the organization.

Patagonia is known for being an unconventional organization. Although in principle they are a global sportswear company, Patagonia is in business to save our home planet. In our conversation with Dean Carter, Patagonia's leader of People and Culture, he talked about how the organization strives to create a courageous and unconventional culture where people can engage in conversations about hard things in a wise and compassionate way. He shared an example of his first experience of wise compassion, when shortly after joining the organization there was an internal debate about footwear. Patagonia shoes were generating millions of dollars in revenue but they realized that at that time, shoes could not be made in a sustainable way that fit their values. After many internal courageous and difficult conversations, they decided to exit footwear, which meant finding new work for the teams formerly engaged in the shoe business. For Dean, "hard things are easier when you are clear on your values. And it is easier for everyone in the organization to find courage over comfort when the organizational values are clear and used as the basis of making visible difficult decisions."

Big, bold, courageous acts by leaders send a strong message to everyone in the organization that it is okay to challenge the status quo—that if you see something you think is not good for the company's success, speak up. Creating courageous cultures is about cultivating a collective recognition that when we individually choose courage over comfort, we all win. As leaders, when we demonstrate courage and reward others for courageous acts, we create a culture that values courageous confrontations and accountability. When you create this type of environment, people can be more creative, and you create more space for greater accountability and higher performance.

Injecting caring courage into your culture puts a healthy pressure on everyone. If a team or team member is not performing well or acting in ways that may not serve the mission, it is the cultural norm to address it. People will feel free and empowered to speak up, even when they disagree. This kind of caring courage, embedded into the culture, creates the foundation for taking the next step in the Wise Compassion Flywheel. As we will explore in the next chapter, with a willingness to embrace courage over comfort we can now work to bring more caring candor to our leadership and our organization.

8

Direct Is Faster

Consider two organizations. In Company A, people are incredibly kind and caring. So much so that people hold back sharing things that would cause dissent or make people uncomfortable. There is a great sense of unity and harmony but a real danger in groupthink, not learning from mistakes, and lack of professional development. Company B is at the opposite end of this spectrum. People speak their mind and share the unvarnished truth without considering the impact on others. They pride themselves on "telling it like it is," even when it might seem cruel. People feel so under the gun they are afraid to take risks and feel at risk of being publicly shamed.

Which company would you want to work for?

Probably neither.

In either extreme of too much care and too much candor, an organization will not be successful. And this is why as leaders we need to find the middle ground where we can balance care and candor to create a kind *and* straight-talking culture. This is caring candor.

Being candid is to say what needs to be said, without beating around the bush. But candor requires care. Otherwise, it is just brutal

FIGURE 8-1

The Wise Compassion Flywheel—caring candor

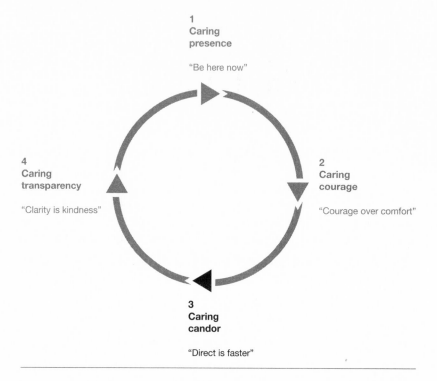

1
Caring
presence

"Be here now"

4
Caring
transparency

"Clarity is kindness"

2
Caring
courage

"Courage over comfort"

3
Caring
candor

"Direct is faster"

honesty. Candor requires courage, too. Without courage we may end up leading from Quadrant 1 (Caring Avoidance) out of fear of offending the other person, or from Quadrant 4 (Uncaring Execution) out of fear of the pain we may experience in being direct with others. In this way, caring candor follows from caring courage on the Wise Compassion Flywheel as shown in figure 8-1.

The mantra for caring candor is "Direct is faster." Being candid is about being direct and straightforward, and it is always faster. With caring candor, you deliver the message in the most kind and direct way, which allows for the other person to receive it quickly and for the real conversation to begin.

The opposite of directness is indirectness or beating around the bush. When we beat around the bush, we make the conversation much more difficult for the people we communicate with. This is unkind. As Ulrika Biesert, CHRO of IKEA, stated, "It's easy to fall for the illusion that we protect people by not being candid with them. When you're not dealing with the situation in a direct way, you are being unkind. You may think that you are being caring, but you're not." When Ulrika is faced with situations that require candor, she always asks herself how she would want to be treated: "I would hate if someone didn't talk candidly to me about what's really happening. I prefer to be treated with the assumption that I am strong enough to embrace directness. I truly believe all of us are the same in this way." Candor is a compliment to the people we're working with. If we are candid, it implies we respect others and speak to them as we would want them to speak to us.

Findings from our global compassionate leadership survey provide insight for leaders in terms of the importance of balancing care and candor as they rise through the executive ranks. As explained earlier, our data shows that as leaders progress, followers perceive them as less wise and less compassionate. In our research, "team leads" were rated as the highest in wisdom and compassion by their followers, whereas "executives" were rated the lowest. Although there are many reasons why this could be true, our hypothesis is that it is because leaders in more progressively senior roles have to make more tough decisions and deliver more difficult messages, which can be seen as being unwise and unkind by followers. Combining care and candor is a vehicle for striving to counteract this perception.

In this chapter, we explain what caring candor looks like, provide more context around why it is difficult to be candid, and provide strategies for how we can bring more caring candor into our leadership.

Caring Candor, Not Brutal Honesty

Candor on its own can easily come across as brutal honesty. With brutal honesty, we show little care for the other person and simply state our unfiltered opinions. Although these can be valid thoughts to share, it is not caring candor; it is uncontrolled thoughtlessness. Caring candor is not a free pass to speak your mind with all the confusion that happens in a heated moment. At the same time, it is also not the process of holding back thoughts, suggestions, or difficult feedback.

Caring candor is like having a hard back and a soft front. The hard back is our strength, confidence, decisiveness, and conviction. It's about knowing our values and showing our people and team the opportunities for improvement. The posture of a hard back is that of standing firm with dignity. The soft front is our openness to other people's perspectives and care for their emotions and well-being. Put together, the hard back helps followers have trust in the direction, and the soft front makes people feel cared for.

This is important because although the value of increasing candor in the workplace is clear, severe candor without compassion can create hostile, ruthless environments where people feel constantly under threat, stress levels are high, and people leave or fail to perform at their best. Again, in this situation, we begin to lead from Quadrant 4 (Uncaring Execution), possibly gaining immediate results, but with decreasing returns over the long run.

To help you reflect on whether how you speak is caring directness or brutal honesty, imagine there is a microphone in the room recording you. Would you be willing to share the recording with the rest of the organization? If you were to modify the recording and be the receiver versus the sender, would you want someone to speak like that to you?

Faster, Smarter, Better

Caring candor is faster. When we beat around the bush and don't get to the point with people, we are wasting everyone's time. When we are direct, we get to the heart of the matter and allow people to engage in the important conversations about what comes next. When we present the issues right from the start of the conversation, we allow the time for people to digest and respond and therefore gain clarity on what needs to be done. Conversely, when we start to wrap hard messages in long-winded, detour-like explanations, we leave people confused about what we are trying to say. If we are not candid, we create an uncomfortable tension for people of knowing that something that should be said is not being said.

Many leaders have a hard time being candid because they feel it comes across as authoritarian. That can certainly be the case, but only if the candor is not caring. If there is care in candor, most of us appreciate getting the input and feedback directly delivered. Jessica Neal, CHRO of Netflix, told us, "When first coming to Netflix and working with Reed Hastings, he was very direct with me. It wasn't negative. He was just honest, candid, and clear. He said, 'You're running your program in a way that won't net the best results, and it would be better if you did X, Y, and Z.' Reed's compassionate and candid feedback helped me to model the same with my teams and further enhance our kind and candid culture."

Jessica walked us through an example of what caring candor looks like for her. She told us about a leader on her team who was very controlling of direct reports. Jessica decided she needed to talk with this leader. She started the conversation with "We need to talk about some things that are going to be hard to hear, and I want you to listen. I want you to know that I'm telling you about these because I care about you and I want you to be successful at Netflix."

At first, the controlling leader had tears in her eyes. She got defensive and wanted to show Jessica text messages from people on her team that said she was the best leader they ever had.

Jessica told her, "I don't need to see those, but I need you to hear the feedback. Both things can be true. Some of them may value you as a leader, but the ones I spoke with are finding it difficult to work with you. So, I need you to be open to this and to try to figure out how you can own what's happening."

By the end of their talk, the team leader was appreciative. She knew that she didn't intend to be seen as controlling and difficult. It wasn't the type of leader she wanted to be, and she was committed to doing something about it. Jessica encouraged her to talk to her team and together look at ways she could help make them feel more empowered and less controlled. This was not easy for the leader, but she could feel that Jessica cared about her and cared about her success at Netflix. This gave her the confidence to go to her team and put the issues on the table.

Jessica continued to follow up with the underperforming leader in a candid and caring manner. "I told her, if we're not progressing, that's not great, and we'll have to determine whether or not she can continue to be a leader here. But if she is progressing, then that's wonderful. It's all about learning. If we stay in the learning mode and if we see progress, and then it's a success story."

In her approach to this situation, Jessica also sent a message to the members of the leader's team on how Netflix values candid feedback. By encouraging the leader to engage her direct reports in her development, Jessica made it clear that creating a culture of candor is the way to enable Netflix to address issues and enhance performance.

Candor Is Kindness

Candor is at the core of development and growth. In this way, being direct with people is one of the kindest things we can do for another. Only by being candid will people get the feedback and input they need to develop and grow and become better. As Jill Ader, chairwoman of Egon Zehnder, affirmed, "A good leader calls out the hero in everyone. Good leadership is to see people's potential and be direct in challenging them with care."

Consider the tough feedback you have received throughout your career. Where would you be today without the people who were kind enough to muster the courage to candidly share their perspectives on your performance with you?

For Mike Vierow, associate partner with McKinsey & Company, wisdom is having the foresight to see the dominoes that are stacking up, and to act in a kind and compassionate way. In his words, "Being candid now is a gift because it creates the potential to make our future easier." Issues are like untreated infections; the longer you leave them, the more the infection spreads, and the more painful it becomes. In leadership, we must deal with issues as they arise. Problems don't get better because you try to convince yourself they don't exist. They fester. Deal with things—and do it quickly and decisively.

If you don't, everyone loses.

Candor Sends the Right Message

When we are not direct in dealing with a situation, we are letting others down in two ways. First, the issue may not be addressed, which can be detrimental to the team. Second, it sends a message to others that "bad" behavior is tolerated. Questions will increase over time—for example, "How come so-and-so is able to act in that way? Why are they able to get away with stuff?" This fosters an environment which can undermine motivation and performance.

In our conversation with Helena Gottschling, CHRO of the Royal Bank of Canada, she spoke about how important it is for leaders to respectfully address issues head on. She shared a story about how she recently got into a heated discussion with a senior leader who did not want to take action with an individual on his team. He was protecting the individual and hoping he could fix him. But the individual had broken organizational rules multiple times. Helena told him, "You're losing credibility as a leader. You are sending a message to the team that it's okay to breach code. It's not okay, and you need to act." When Helena helped the leader see the impact his nonaction was having on the rest of the organization, he was able to let go.

One of the things we heard from many of the leaders we interviewed was the risk of making someone's performance issues a personal reflection on us. We don't want to face the issues in their performance because we are afraid it will reflect badly on our leadership. As Helena noted, this can be particularly true for senior leaders because the people they appoint are in high-profile, complex, strategic positions. It can be more difficult to admit that this person you promoted or hired into this extremely important role is not up for the task. In reality, when we are direct in dealing with situations, we address issues faster and send the right message to the people within the organization regarding what is expected.

Don't Wrap a Hand Grenade

When we have a difficult message, the most natural thing to do is to try to soften it. As we have explored throughout this book, because we are good people and we don't want to hurt others, we can fall into a trap of wrapping hard messages so they don't sound so bad. This is unkind. When you have a difficult message, the kindest and most skillful thing to do is to present it as directly as possible. In other words, don't wrap a hand grenade.

Consider the two following scenarios:

- Your boss stops by your desk to tell you that you are doing a great job and that she appreciates your hard work. She adds, "Too bad that presentation to ACME Widgets didn't land so well, but no big deal. Overall, we're still on track. Keep up the great work." Then she walks away.

- You are having an informal catch-up with your boss, and he says, "What a great job Sam is doing. Sam is really stepping up to the plate. We're so lucky to have him on the team. Wouldn't it be great if we had more people like Sam?"

Reflect for a moment on how these scenarios would make you feel. Probably not very good. In the first scenario, you likely already knew the presentation didn't go very well. Since you are still moving forward, however, you probably didn't think it was a big deal. But now you aren't so sure. Should you be reading between the lines? If so, what's the real message? In the second scenario, sure, you know Sam is a superstar. And, of course, it would be great to have more people like Sam. But is the real message that you should start looking for a new job because you clearly pale in comparison to Sam?

Now, consider your own example of a time when a leader shared something you thought might have been critical feedback, but you weren't sure. Perhaps the message was couched between a lot of praise. Or maybe it was so indirect you weren't sure it was even about you. You may have gone home that day ruminating over whether you should do something or not. Should you ask some additional questions? Should you update your résumé?

When we conceal hard messages, it is equivalent to wrapping a hand grenade. It may make us feel better because we are softening something difficult, but it can leave the receiver confused and uneasy. Instead, when we have tough messages, we need to have the courage to be direct. We need to relay our message as simply and plainly as possible. If you deliver the equivalent of an emotional hand grenade, have the kindness and respect to ensure that the recipient sees it for what it is. Though it may feel harsh, it is, in fact, the kind thing to do. Then, at least, they know what they have just received.

Minding the Landmines

If we are launching the equivalent of emotional hand grenades, we need to be prepared to deal with the emotional landmines. We are emotional beings, and the reason why hard things are hard is because they trigger our emotions. To trigger as few emotional landmines as possible, caring candor requires that we are mindful of what we say, how we say it, and when we say it. We also need to ensure we are well prepared to respond constructively to negative emotions when and if they arise.

Being mindful of emotional landmines requires concise and thoughtful communication. When delivering tough messages, it is critical to choose your words carefully. As leaders, we sometimes underestimate the power of our words. One simple, flippant comment can create ripples of confusion or frustration. Caring candor is about paying close attention to what we communicate, so that we don't do unintentional harm.

But regardless of how hard we try, in doing hard things, there is always potential for miscommunication and misunderstanding. Therefore, we need to notice when someone gets triggered by something we say. Noticing when someone has been triggered and then creating space to process it can help de-escalate an emotionally charged conversation and enable it to become an opportunity for development and learning. This requires presence, courage, and directness. It requires presence to notice that a person may have been triggered, courage to say something about it, and directness to address it in a candid way.

Consider Culture Differences

Caring candor is faster. But if you forget to factor in cultural differences, it can be much slower. Erin Meyer, author of *The Culture Map*, argues that one of the distinguishing factors between cultures is their level of directness.[1] For example, according to her research, people from the Netherlands are among the most direct in the world. They do not beat around the bush, but generally get straight to the matter and say what needs to be said. Between Dutch people, this is considered normal and culturally acceptable, and therefore among each other they can be quick in getting to the core of the matter without taking any offense.

But for a British person, the Dutch directness can be challenging. Though the Dutch are considered among the most direct, the British are the exact opposite. Therefore, if a Dutch person is not culturally sensitive and speaks with Dutch directness, it could be considered rude, arrogant, and unkind in the ears of a Brit. This in turn will make it unlikely that the British person will be open to the message. In the same way, if a British person gives feedback to a Dutch person, the Dutch person is likely to miss the message because it can be wrapped in too many so-called downgraders. Downgraders are phrases like "kind of," "sort of," "a little bit," and "perhaps" that serve to soften criticism.

Who is right in their approach, the Dutch person or the British person? They both are. From their own cultural perspective, they are both correct in their approach. Within their own cultures, their ways of communicating work perfectly well. But when working with colleagues and clients from other cultures, it is important to understand their cultural norms for directness. If not, being direct can actually slow the process.

When we are caring and candid, we are able to be direct, but in a way that respects the person in front of us, being mindful of potential cultural differences. The following are practical strategies for bringing more caring candor into your leadership.

Strategies for Caring Candor

Bringing care and candor into your leadership is a discipline that takes practice. There is a fine line between being perceived as a leader who is from Company A and seen as nice but ineffective, versus being from Company B and seen as brutally honest, verging on being cruel. The following strategies can help.

STRATEGIES FOR CULTIVATING CARING CANDOR

- Be mindful of the setting and context.
- Say it now and do it quickly.
- Bottom line it first.
- Be firm and decisive.
- Avoid the popularity game.
- Have zero tolerance for value breakers.

Strategy 1: Be Mindful of the Setting and Context

Candid messages can be hard for the receiver to hear. Candid messages delivered in a setting that creates potential for making them even harder to hear can be unwise and unkind. Being mindful of the setting and context means that you consider when, where, and how you are going to share a candid message. This is true when you are planning a candid message in advance but also important when something comes up in the moment. When you see something that needs to be shared, pause before saying what is on your mind to ensure that the setting and context are conducive to your message being received.

One of the most important considerations is whether the message is delivered in public or private. Stories abound of leaders like Steve Jobs or Jack Welch who were known for routinely berating people in public. And there are those who would argue that this can be helpful because it makes it clear to the individual and others what behavior is acceptable and what is not. At the same time, we know that from an emotional and social perspective, public shaming can feel heartless and cruel to the recipient as well as the observers. The key is to remember that caring candor is not just speaking your mind. It is about being mindful and giving due consideration to the setting and context before choosing when and how to bring candor to the table. And when in doubt, in most instances, candid conversations have the most care when delivered in private and one to one.

Strategy 2: Say It Now and Do It Quickly

When we need to do hard things, it is human nature to find ways to put them off. But procrastination does not serve anyone. Remember that waiting will only make it harder. Rather than putting hard things off, make a habit of quick action to tackle issues that need to be addressed. When you see something or hear something, act right away. The more you act swiftly, the more you will get used to it. It will become more natural for you and for the people you work with. Also, importantly, people will start to realize that you are always swift in addressing issues, which will give them confidence in your leadership.

Note that in line with the first strategy, taking action does not necessarily mean calling someone out in public. It could mean following up immediately after a meeting and asking for a quick conversation. Being quick to act serves to keep the context relevant for both you and the other person. It helps avoid situations where there are disagreements about what was said. It also serves to avoid situations where someone says, "Why didn't you tell me sooner?"

Strategy 3: Bottom Line It First

Being upfront about the "bottom line" is a way to bring more care and candor to your communication. Bottom lining it first means that you start with the conclusion—that is, the key message that needs to be shared—and then provide the context, versus the other way around. In other words, you get straight to the point. If the person is going to be let go, or the project is going to be canceled, or you need to give them some tough feedback, lead with this. This approach lets people know immediately what the conversation is about, giving them context. Otherwise, they may be sitting there thinking, *Where's this conversation going?* Or, *Why are you telling me these things?*

Being upfront about the bottom line helps to ensure you don't spend time wrapping a hand grenade. As noted above, if you have something difficult to share, it's best to be direct so that you can look at it together. Trying to ease into a difficult message is generally only serving to make it easier for you, not easier for the other person. Tell them what you need to tell them and then focus on the background, details, or next steps. Although it may seem harsh to jump in with a tough message, is it really that much better when it comes at the end?

Strategy 4: Be Firm and Decisive

When being direct in delivering a difficult message to someone, be firm and decisive. If you are firing someone, be clear in your language and say, "It is my decision to . . ." rather than vaguely saying, "I think it is better if . . ." When firing someone, you are not opening up a negotiation—you are taking a decisive action. It is compassionate to make that clear from the beginning, so the other person can focus on next steps instead of trying to debate or negotiate. Being firm and decisive creates clear parameters for the other person to navigate the new situation. This is much more human and compassionate than being vague and unclear.

Strategy 5: Avoid the Popularity Game

As leaders we must avoid the popularity game. We have to make many decisions that are benefiting the greater good and therefore can be difficult for individuals. As a result, we may or may not always be liked. But leadership is not about being liked. It is about being respected for doing the right things that serve the greater good. This is difficult, because we all have a part of us that wants to please others and wants to be seen in a positive light.

If, as a leader, you have a strong bias for being liked, it can easily result in decisions that are not in the best interest of individuals or an organization. If you want to be successful, you must abandon the popularity game and strive to be respected.

Dave Conder, head of global talent at KPMG, spoke with us about the two types of worries leaders have when doing hard things: "healthy worries" and "unhealthy worries." As he shared, healthy worries include the consideration of how people will take a tough message and what impact it will have on their lives. Unhealthy worries are concerns about becoming unpopular. Always ask yourself: Am I worried for myself or worried about others?

Do not expect that by bringing more compassion into your leadership, you will be liked. You can do all of the right things in all of the right ways and still be resented. Just get over it. Compassion is not a way of being popular. We have this ideal concept of the beloved leader. But leadership is not always like that. And the fact that people resent you or don't like what you're doing does not make you wrong. You just need to have the inner strength to be confident about your belief that you have done the right thing. That is your anchor. You have to have a strong inner conviction as a leader to not need the approval of others, even when you are trying to care for them.

Strategy 6: Have Zero Tolerance for Value Breakers

Directness is important in all aspects of leadership, but the most important area is to be direct and fast in addressing issues related to breach of values or cultural norms. If we want people to have confidence in the values we espouse, we need to be direct in how we deal with people who operate against those values. When we have zero tolerance for value breakers, it sends a clear message to all employees that we are serious about our values. It also makes it easier for others in the organization to act in ways that are aligned with those values because they have greater clarity on the boundaries.

Henrik Ehrnrooth, CEO of KONE, shared some advice he received early in his career from another CEO: "Never think or expect that people don't see what decisions you should be making. As a leader everybody's eyes are on you. And people see clearer than you what you do and what you are not doing that you should do. If you are not rock solid in directly addressing breaches of cultural and value norms in the company, people will lose respect for you and engagement in their work."

Candor Creates Clarity

When we can be candid with each other, issues that need to be discussed surface easily and are discussed. In our conversation with

Narayana Murthy, founder and former CEO of Infosys, one of the values he instilled in the company was "let the good news take the stairs, but ensure bad news always takes the elevator." In other words, good news can be delivered at the normal pace of communication, but bad news must be fast-tracked. People must be encouraged to share it and share it immediately in simple and direct words. This is why being direct is so important—it is faster. When we have a culture of candor, we create the space for more transparency in which relevant information is more freely shared. And, as you'll see in the next chapter, making candor part of your culture enhances clarity and provides the basis for greater trust and psychological safety.

9

Clarity Is Kindness

Early in his career at Eli Lilly and Company, David A. Ricks, now chairman and CEO, was confronted with a big challenge. While he was leading the Canadian affiliate of the company, a key product equating to almost half of its revenue lost intellectual property protection. Try to imagine the situation: key leaders and employees are looking to you for answers about the future of the business and their own livelihood. You have very few options, answers, or solutions. What do you do?

Dave knew that the right approach was to be straightforward and transparent with employees—even if there was very little information to provide at that moment. So, he held a town hall and gave everyone the opportunity to ask questions. He wasn't able to answer questions about the future of the business. He could not make any commitments about job security. He could not say whether there would be layoffs. And he could not say when he would have more answers. It wasn't that he was trying to hide anything. He simply did not know. Dave did believe the best approach was to stand up, face people, and be clear about the uncertainty. When interviewing Dave for this book, he said, "I had to face people looking for guidance and direction. They had to make some personal choices without having clear answers. It was hard. It was very uncomfortable. But it was a good lesson, because it was the right thing to do." Dave knew it was not only the right thing to do, it was the most compassionate thing to do. "Employees were entitled to have a transparent view of the future," he said. "With that honest view, I knew that they would be able to better plan their lives."

Being transparent is about sharing relevant information, not having secrets, and letting people know who you are and what you stand for. Transparency is distinct from candor in that you can be candid and still conceal information. When you are transparent, people know what is on your mind. And when you add caring to transparency, people also know what is in your heart.

Caring transparency makes people feel safe. It creates an environment of trust and psychological safety. This is the fourth step in the Wise Compassion Flywheel (figure 9-1) because caring transparency relies on a foundation of presence, courage, and candor.

We need to be present, courageous, and candid to open up ourselves and the organization to create more transparency. And with caring transparency we can create a culture in which people have confidence in and respect for who you are, what you say, and what you do.

The mantra for caring transparency is "Clarity is kindness." When people know what they need to know and see you for who you are, things are clear. This is in contrast to when things are cloudy and opaque. When there is a lack of clarity in a work setting, it can create a culture of confusion and distrust. When we remember that clarity is kindness—people like to be able to see things for what they really are—we bring more caring transparency to our leadership and culture.

In this chapter, we look at why clarity is kindness and the benefits of caring transparency. We then explore how caring transparency leads to greater trust and psychological safety.

FIGURE 9-1

The Wise Compassion Flywheel—caring transparency

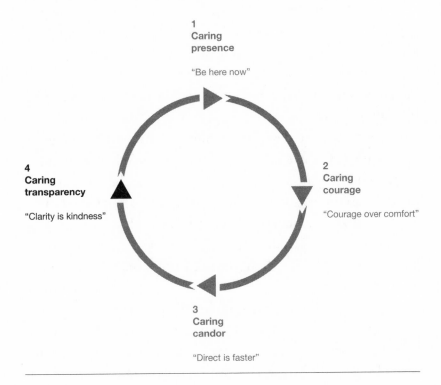

1
Caring
presence

"Be here now"

4
**Caring
transparency**

"Clarity is kindness"

2
Caring
courage

"Courage over comfort"

3
Caring
candor

"Direct is faster"

Caring Transparency for Clear Communication

Caring transparency is the quality of being open and honest about what is on our minds and in our hearts. This includes getting ideas and thoughts out in the open—to make the invisible visible. When being transparent, we provide all available and shareable details so that people know where they stand and what comes next. Clarity and transparency are the opposite of obscurity and secrecy. When you don't share all the details, you leave people in the dark. They have no choice but to second guess, ruminate, and worry. A lack of clarity only leads to unhappiness and anxiety. It causes people's imaginations to run wild, their minds spinning and colored by fear and negativity.

It is a fundamental human need to know. Knowing is power. Knowing gives us the outlook to find our path in life and ultimately survive. Therefore, when speaking with caring transparency, we are not holding back important information out of fear of how it will be received or out of fear of how we will be perceived if we don't have all the answers.

Just as with directness, being transparent requires courage. It takes courage to share information that people might not want to hear, even if they need to hear it. By not telling the full truth, we might be able to convince ourselves that we're being kind. But instead, what we're actually doing is being unkind and unfair. Sure, feeding people half-truths may make them feel better. But this is almost always about making ourselves feel more comfortable, which is unkind.

As leaders we cannot overestimate the power of sharing information and creating a sense of transparency for our people. It nourishes them on a fundamental level. Transparency makes people thrive because they *know*. Not sharing information is the same as leaving people blindfolded to navigate an unknown territory. It is not just unkind, it is unwise. Transparency is the fairest and most humane approach to leadership, yet it is not easy because it often includes sharing things people don't want to hear. Because of this, transparency is the foundation for effective communication and trusting relationships.

Clarity, Kindness, and Transparency Enable Trust

Trust enables people to work together and work through hardships. If people know you care about them and have their backs, it will be a lot easier for them to hear a difficult message. If they know you will tell them things they need to hear and not hold back, they will have more confidence in you and in your leadership. These are the foundations of healthy, trusting relationships.

And this is critical in any organization, but especially in today's work context where many people work remotely and have limited social connection. Many people are working in teams with leaders and coworkers they have never met in person. From a neurological perspective, this is tough, especially when it comes to building and maintaining trust. We are less likely to trust someone we don't know. We are also less likely to trust someone we don't see on a regular basis. And if there is something difficult that needs to be discussed, if that message needs to be delivered remotely, it makes it even more difficult to create a sense of care and connection.

We know that the future of work will continue to include a high degree of remote work. We also know that the future of any business will continue to have a high degree of volatility. This means that it will be harder to cultivate trust and that there will be more hard messages that need to be delivered due to constant change. The bottom line is that proactively cultivating the foundation for trusting relationships will be more important than ever.

There are three core elements of building and maintaining trusting relationships. The first is connection, which requires presence. As explored in chapter 6, presence means that we are being attentive, open, and curious, which creates the foundation for trust. The second element is compassion. If I believe you care about me and have the intention to be of benefit, it allows me to let down my guard and be trusting. The third element is credibility, which is about ethical behavior and doing what you say you are going to do. When we connect, when I know you care and I have confidence in your conduct, it creates space for trust. Although things may be challenging between us, I have a clear sense of who you are, what you stand for, and that you care about me. This is the essence of caring transparency. This platform of trust enables us to step into the hard elements of workplace human dynamics with something solid to fall back on when things get difficult. In this way, building and establishing trust through clarity and transparency provides the foundation for developing psychological safety.

Transparency Creates Psychological Safety

Wise compassionate leadership creates a culture of psychological safety and inclusion. Why? Because compassion makes people feel safe and that their leaders have their backs. Amy Edmondson, professor of leadership and management at Harvard Business School, has been widely acknowledged as one of the foremost researchers on psychological safety at work. Her focus in this area started by accident. She was studying medical teams and assessing factors that contributed to reduction in errors when she made an interesting discovery. Some teams appeared to have higher error rates than others, causing her at first to conclude that they must have greater deficiencies that would result in more negative outcomes. To her surprise, she discovered that those with higher error rates were more comfortable sharing potential issues than the other teams. The teams with more open discussions of error, she hypothesized, would have better outcomes not worse—a speculation that would have to be formally tested in later research. Edmondson had discovered something more fundamental about the work climate: a team's willingness to share concerns without fear of reprisal meant its members would be able to address issues before they became problems. In contrast, teams that had more hierarchical relationships, especially between nurses and doctors, were at risk of valuable and potentially lifesaving concerns not being shared.

Beyond avoiding medical errors, Edmondson and others have demonstrated many benefits for cultivating psychological safety in work teams. In her book *The Fearless Organization*, Edmondson shares examples of how psychological safety enables faster adoption of new technologies, faster adaptation to new market circumstances and customer requirements, early identification of potentially catastrophic risks, and the development of innovative products.

One widely cited study that enhanced understanding of the power of psychological safety in teams was called Project Aristotle, done by Google. The study identified five critical traits of high-performing teams and found that psychological safety was the most foundational of these traits.[1] That is, without psychological safety, you cannot have a high-performing team. Project Aristotle found that psychological safety is strongly associated with objective (e.g., sales revenue) and subjective (e.g., ratings of team performance by team members and managers or customer satisfaction with team products) indicators of team performance.

The link between compassion and psychological safety should be obvious. If we create a condition in which our employees genuinely feel we care, it is a foundation for creating a safe environment. But it's insufficient. In fact, an environment where everyone is merely kind and caring about each other can make it more difficult for people to raise concerns, because they don't want to break the social cohesion. This would be a culture that is operating out of Quadrant 1 (Caring Avoidance); people are kind but avoid sharing information that might offend.

Therefore, it is important to inject wisdom into the culture. People need to be encouraged to have the courage to bring their best mind to the table and speak up for the betterment of the team. At the same time, being too direct and too blunt about things that are wrong can create an environment of fear of reprisal and again create an environment where people don't speak up. That is why we need the combination of wisdom and compassion. As Professor Edmondson told us, "Wise compassion is essential to psychological safety. Without wise compassion, the culture suffers because no one feels safe to speak up. No one will share their thoughts. As a leader, you are therefore cut off from getting the information you need to skillfully navigate your business and your team."

When people do speak up, it should be celebrated. But this is not easy. In a work setting, identifying risks or raising concerns makes us afraid that we will not be seen as a team player or perceived as averse to change. If we ask too many questions, we may fear looking foolish. Challenging authority and going against the group generates interpersonal risks that threaten our social safety. Though many leaders encourage dissenting views and strive to create a learning culture, creating an environment where people feel safe to be socially vulnerable is challenging. We have an inherent fear of social rejection. None of us want to be kicked out of the tribe.

So, what can we do?

One important point to understand is that psychological safety doesn't just come about out of nowhere. It is an organizational outcome that emerges when all the necessary ingredients are present ahead of time, both between leaders and followers and embedded in the culture. In other words, it is something that needs to be continually developed over time. A recent meta-analysis and summary paper on psychological safety documented all known inputs and found that "positive leader relations" was one of the biggest contributors to psychological safety in the workplace.[2] This highlights the importance of compassionate leadership as the foundation for an ongoing journey, in shaping the work context and the integral role that leaders play in building a psychologically safe culture.

The journey toward greater compassionate leadership starts with presence, then courage, then candor, and lands when we create a culture of caring transparency. The following section shares how to bring more caring transparency into your leadership and culture.

Strategies to Enhance Caring Transparency

Clarity, transparency, and a resulting culture of psychological safety can be nurtured in many ways. The following are practical strategies for implementing a cycle of caring transparency and psychological safety.

STRATEGIES FOR ENHANCING CARING TRANSPARENCY

- Strive for clarity as a state of mind.
- Treat people as adults.
- Seek clarity to enhance clarity.
- Make time for connection.
- Encourage dissent.
- Demonstrate humility.
- Show your true self.

Strategy 1: Strive for Clarity as a State of Mind

If we want to bring more transparency to our leadership, we need to start with a clear mind. When our mind is cluttered, we cannot think clearly or see clearly. Most of us spend our days rushing from meeting to meeting with brief spaces in between filled with responding to messages or putting out fires. This way of working builds a lot of mental clutter.

Taking mindful breaks throughout the day to clear the mental clutter is a great way to create more clarity for ourselves and enables us to be clearer and more transparent with others. Taking time to pause before sending a message or starting a meeting is also a way to ensure what you are sending or saying is as clear as possible. This is kindness. Consider how much confusion has occurred and how much time has been wasted in your organization because an email was unclear or meeting objectives were not clearly defined.

Clarity as a state of mind is also about having a discipline of being clear and concise in your communication. Thinking about what you want to say and ensuring you are sharing what needs to be said in the best way possible enhance communication. Clarity is also about simplification. As wisely stated by the artist Hans Hoffman, "The ability to simplify means to eliminate the unnecessary so that the necessary may speak." In other words, less is more.

When doing hard things, helping people understand what you are saying is key. To ensure what you are saying is clear, it is better to have short, crisp messages. If a message is long-winded, the main point can get lost and people might leave confused and lost.

When we clear the mental clutter, it is like clearing the room of things that can get in the way of positive human connection. When there is less clutter, you are less distracted, and it is easier for people to see through you and feel more comfortable in your presence. A clear state of mind enables us to be more caring and transparent.

Strategy 2: Treat People as Adults

Being transparent means treating people like you would want to be treated. In the anecdote that opens this chapter, when Dave Ricks stood up and addressed his employees and shared the reality of their situation, he treated them as he would want to be treated. He did not withhold information, but rather trusted that they would prefer to hear the hard news right away rather than waiting until he had more answers.

When we withhold information, we are not showing respect to the people who work for us—because we take away their chances of planning their lives accordingly.

Dave provided the full story of what had happened and what was going on, and did not make any commitments about job security or what the future may hold. He shared openly that there were many things he did not know. While that can be deeply concerning for some people, it was true. And when it comes to our work, we need to know what is really happening and not default to wishful thinking.

Wise compassionate leadership means treating people as adults—with full transparency and clarity, combined with care—so that they know exactly where they stand and can plan their lives based on reality.

Strategy 3: Seek Clarity to Enhance Clarity

It is one thing to have a goal of creating a more transparent culture where information is more freely shared. But in any exchange of information, there is a sender and one or more receivers. And, as we all know, the information you send may or may not be the information I receive. As Alan Greenspan, former chair of the Federal Reserve of the United States, stated, "I know you think you understand what you thought I said, but I'm not sure you realize that what you heard is not what I meant."

As leaders we need to remember that communication is a two-way street. We need to create mechanisms to ensure what we shared is clearly understood. This requires that we don't make assumptions and, instead, ask questions. When dealing with hard things, this means spending more time in a space that is uncomfortable. But it is critical. And it is also a sign of respect. When we take the time to ensure that others have understood what we've shared, it shows we care about them. It shows that as difficult as this conversation may be, we're willing to stay in it until we're sure everything is clear and properly understood.

This willingness to make time for clarity creates space for richer and deeper conversations and relationships.

Strategy 4: Make Time for Connection

Creating a sense of caring transparency is greatly enhanced when we are intentional about making time just to connect. When we connect as human beings, we create greater caring transparency because people see us as a whole person and feel more comfortable in our presence. Human beings have a much more difficult time connecting with people they don't know, and it is more difficult to get to know someone we have never met in person.

In today's virtual, remote workspace, we need to be much more intentional in making time to connect. This can take many forms, including check-ins at the beginning of meetings, informal virtual cafés, online social activities, or structured exercises facilitated online or in person. The key thing is to make time for it and make sure the time is well spent. If people think it is a waste of time or feel they are forced to participate, it will not be of benefit.

These moments of human connection should not be underestimated. We are social beings, and we work better together and enjoy work more together when we feel connected. In our increasingly virtual workplace, we need to be intentional about creating moments for real and transparent human connection.

Paul Daugherty is the chief technology officer at Accenture and author of the book *Human and Machine: Reimagining Work in the Age of AI*. Although Paul is passionate about technology and everything it can do for us, when we spoke with him, he stressed the importance of creating real human connections. "Humans need and want human interaction," he told us. "As leaders, we need to find ways to invest in the relationship bank account with our people." In his view, "All businesses are technology businesses, and leaders need to understand that. But ultimately, it is our ability to cultivate meaningful human connections that allows a business to thrive."

Strategy 5: Encourage Dissent

Most leaders will say they want people to share concerns, raise objections, and point out issues. But creating this type of environment is not easy. To encourage people to share concerns and ask questions, it needs to be part of the culture. From a wise compassionate perspective, this means people feel safe to disagree and have confidence that when they raise objections, they will be celebrated instead of rejected.

Ways to create a culture of dissent include being mindful of language. For example, consider the innocent question a leader may pose in a meeting: "Does everyone agree?" The unintended signal this leader is sending is that everyone should agree. So, even if the leader is genuinely open to challenge, members of the team may not feel comfortable speaking up. A better question may be, "Who would like to share why this is a bad idea?"

It is also important to create structures to ensure that dissenting views are brought to the table. For example, asking everyone to share three reasons why an idea won't work is better than asking an open generic question (and one that may be potentially interpersonally risky) inviting anyone to share a dissenting view. Also, it can be helpful to invite people to share opposing views anonymously.

Research has found that when leaders and organizations push back against dissent, they breed a toxic workplace culture built on bad actors and a silencing of principled dissent.[3] Through creating the right incentives, leaders who give voice to caring and motivated employees willing to share dissenting views ultimately contribute to individual and organizational well-being. Open and productive dissenters are often integral to business success due to a diversity of thought that drives innovation and because they tend to retain the most talented, productive, and loyal employees. Many leaders take the steps of encouraging dissent, but rarely follow up by engaging with the dissenting views and celebrating the person who spoke up. Both are important to reinforce the message that dissent is truly welcomed. When we encourage dissent, engage in the conversation, and celebrate when people are brave enough to share tough messages, we create a culture of greater transparency. The invisible becomes visible—and not only in terms of what people can see in us, but what we can see in others. This creates a culture where people are not holding back, where people share what is not working, and where people are more comfortable taking risks and making mistakes.

Strategy 6: Demonstrate Humility

In our conversation with Stuart Henderson, client account lead for Accenture in North America, we asked him what lesson he wished he had learned earlier in his career. Without hesitation he said, "That I would be wrong a lot." For Stuart, leaders need to be humble. "You will need advice. You will be wrong, and you will make mistakes. You need to be humble about your mistakes and use them as an opportunity to learn, so you can grow as a leader and a human being." Wisdom in leadership is about being humble, recognizing your limitations, admitting when you don't know the answer, and being open about your mistakes. When we can bring humility to our team, we create space for our people to step up and for the entire team to move forward, stronger and smarter together.

Stephanie Lundquist, former CHRO and executive vice president at Target, shared a story with us. She had just started in a new leadership role during a time of significant change and disruption. "It was a challenging situation," she said. "I was honest about what

I thought I knew. But I was also transparent and honest about what I didn't know. And it gave me a great chance to allow others to step in, collaborate, contribute, and help." She realized that by demonstrating humility, it allowed other experts within the organization to rise up and lead. Her willingness to be transparent and humble gave others the space to grow.

Being clear and transparent about your own limitations creates safety for others to ask questions and share their own questions or concerns. When we demonstrate humility, we show that we are human. When we are comfortable with saying "I don't know," we show that it is okay to be wrong and to not have all the answers. And when we openly admit that we made a mistake, we create a culture where others can take risks and feel safe making mistakes. Although for many of us, being vulnerable about what we don't know is hard, ultimately it is a gift because it enables us to show more of our true self.

Strategy 7: Show Your True Self

When delivering tough messages, we have a tendency to put up a shield to protect ourselves from potential backlash from the recipient. Although this protective barrier is natural, it gets in the way of having a heart-to-heart, human-to-human conversation. To develop caring transparency, you need to lower this barrier and allow people to see you as a human being—not as a boss or a leader, but as someone who cares.

Noah Rabinowitz, chief learning officer at Intel, shared with us that he doesn't understand why people talk about their professional selves and their personal selves as if they are different people. "I don't believe you can actually be two people," he told us. "You can behave differently, but you're only one person." In his view, when we try to be someone else, it hinders everything from creativity, to engagement, to innovation, to trust, making it, in his words, "a miserable way to live." To Noah, we are the best leaders when we can be ourselves and lead from a place of who we truly are. This approach is backed by research, with studies finding that leaders who embrace a more authentic leadership style have employees who feel safer in the workplace.[4]

One of the positive elements of the global pandemic was that many of us got to experience our colleagues and leaders in their homes, with their kids or pets running around in the background. One leader we spoke with shared a story of how during a really challenging team meeting, her three-year-old ran through the background without pants. Understandably, her first reaction was embarrassment. But she soon noticed a change in the dynamics of the call. People were more at ease, the heaviness of the discussion was lifted, and someone made a joke about how they might want to consider employing the naked child to run a marketing campaign due to his boldness. Upon reflection, the leader realized that too often she had put up a shield of being the boss and being in control. She was now able to let that go. And when she did, the team opened up and even volunteered to take on tasks that would usually fall to her.

In our desire to treat others as human beings, we can never forget our own humanity. When we allow other people to see our true, authentic selves, it creates space for greater connection, builds trust, and improves teamwork.

Transparency Leads to Presence

Creating a culture of caring transparency opens the space for wisdom and compassion. When the invisible is made visible, people can share difficult issues in a kind and caring way so that people are seen and heard.

The great thing about bringing more transparency into our leadership and culture is that it becomes easier for us to be more present. When we aren't dwelling on information we aren't sharing, it is easier for us to be here now. And when people trust that we are being authentic and telling them what they need to know, it is easier for them to be more present with us. In this way, greater caring transparency leads to caring presence—and this creates momentum for the Wise Compassion Flywheel to spin.

In his bestselling book *Good to Great*, author Jim Collins described the Flywheel Effect as the process of slowly building momentum until there's a sudden breakthrough that allows the wheel to turn faster and faster on its own. With wise compassionate leadership, the cycle is similar. In developing wise compassionate leadership skills, there is no single defining action, no one perfect decision, no miracle moment. Instead, the process is like pushing the heavy flywheel, slowly building momentum until the point of breakthrough. It's a continuum of positive interactions, small successes in which the sum of the parts is greater than the individual moments or solitary actions. And as colleagues, team members, and reports experience wise compassionate leadership in action, the impact becomes exponential.

Soon, other people in your organization will show more wisdom and compassion. Then more will. On and on, until it becomes an ingrained part of your organization's culture, with wise compassionate leadership driving higher levels of performance and producing greater results. In the next chapter, we will pull from key concepts presented throughout the book to share practical insights for how to spin the flywheel in navigating difficult conversations.

The Only Way Out
Is Through

Throughout this book, we have talked about how hard it is to do hard things. We have talked about the challenges of doing hard things in a human way. And now, we will finally reveal how to make doing hard things easy. Are you ready?

Don't worry, it's simple.

Practice.

Sorry if we disappointed you, but in the complex dynamics of navigating hard things, the only way out is through—and by *through*, we mean through doing. We become more skillful at doing hard things by stepping into a difficult situation and coming out on the other side with a little more wisdom and a little more compassion. Over time, it becomes easier. We promise. Every time you go into the territory of doing hard things, if you take time to reflect on what went well and what you will do differently next time, you become wiser.

In other words, now it's time to spin the Wise Compassion Flywheel. We've explored presence. We've discussed courage. We've explained candor. We've unpacked transparency and its connection to psychological safety. Now it's time to put it all into motion by going through the process of wise compassion. Not once. Not twice. But over and over. We can do this by willfully and readily embracing discomfort and having all those hard conversations we've been dreading and deferring.

Through our research, we've had the privilege of interviewing hundreds of C-suite executives. We invited them to share their experiences with doing hard things and the lessons they wished they'd learned earlier in their careers. In this chapter, we want to share insights from their collective years of experience as well as our own learnings from working with senior leaders for the past fifteen years. The rubber truly hits the road for wise compassionate leadership when you have difficult conversations. Entering confrontational situations head on, person-to-person, is the most challenging experience that most leaders face.

In having difficult conversations, we need all the mindsets and skill sets shared throughout this book. We must recognize our common humanity; focus on the greater good; connect with empathy but lead with compassion; apply self-care; overcome busyness; and be present, courageous, candid, and transparent. Bringing these all together enables us to operate from Quadrant 2 of our leadership matrix and be a wiser and more compassionate leader.

Although there are many kinds of difficult conversations, in this chapter we make a distinction between two types: terminal conversations (something is ending) and developmental conversations (something needs to change). They're both tough messages to deliver. Terminal conversations are objectively more difficult, so we classify these as "hard." Developmental conversations are challenging, but not as difficult in terms of their impact on people. These we classify as "feedback." In this chapter, we first look at strategies for how to have "good" hard conversations, that is, how to do them well. Then we examine practical strategies for how to have "good" feedback conversations.

Good Hard Conversations

The most difficult type of conversation happens when you know it will inflict pain on the other person. The pain can be financial, social, or emotional, and in some cases all three. The most obvious example of this is having to let someone go. Telling someone that they no longer have a job is final—there is financial pain, as well as social pain from being kicked out of the tribe. This is the most difficult type of conversation most leaders will need to face. Other conversations that inflict pain include telling someone that they did not get the promotion they were expecting or that the project they have poured their heart and soul into is being shelved. In this section, we will explore strategies for how to have these kinds of conversations with wisdom and compassion.

Before diving into strategies for having a good hard conversation, take a moment to reflect on a time when you were on the receiving end of a poorly delivered tough message.

- Reflect on the experience.

- What was the context?

- What did the person say, or not say, that made the experience bad?

- What could the person have done to make it less brutal?

- Take a moment to write down any reflections.

- Take a few breaths and let go of this negative experience.

Now consider a time when you were on the receiving end of a well-delivered tough message. Again, reflect on the experience.

- What did the person do or not do, say or not say, that made the experience good?

- Take a moment to write down any reflections.

Most likely, we all have similar reflections. In the conversation that did not go well, you probably wrote down things like "the person was not prepared," "they danced around the message," "they were distracted," or "it seemed like they couldn't wait to get out of the room." In the conversations that went well, you probably wrote down things such as "the person was well prepared," "they were upfront and clear in their message," "they were present and calm," "they were kind," or "they were genuinely concerned about the impact this decision had on me."

The point of this exercise is that we all know what bad and good hard conversations look like. And yet, learning how to do them well is an ongoing journey. To help make your journey a little easier, the following are key strategies that will help.

KEYS TO "GOOD" HARD CONVERSATIONS

- Be prepared.
- See others as human beings.
- Give people options.
- Respond—don't react.
- Give time.

Let's take a closer look at each of these strategies.

Strategy 1: Be Prepared

Being prepared sounds obvious. But in our conversations with leaders, they emphasized that no matter how many times you have done these conversations, you must take time and put effort into your preparations. It shows respect for the person you're impacting. This most basic preparation includes thinking through issues like the following:

- What will you say?

- How will you say it?

- What questions might come up?

- How will you respond to those questions?

- Then consider all of the "what happens if . . ." scenarios.

Most organizations have helpful guidelines and support for this type of preparation. But beyond the basics, it is important to be mentally prepared. You have to be prepared for these conversations to feel difficult and be hard. And you also need to stay empathetic with the person and what they're experiencing. To help create optimal conditions for you and those impacted, the following are some additional preparation tips.

- **Plan the Day:** There are a lot of important factors to consider when planning how and where you will have a difficult conversation. Think through what will be most compassionate for the person. Dave Ricks, chairman and CEO of Eli Lilly and Company, shared with us that he always plans to have difficult conversations early in the day: "Otherwise, it feels pretty crappy to let someone go after they have just worked all day." These are small things. But when doing hard things, the little stuff counts. A few other little details to consider include the following: Don't be late, don't be rushed, and ensure that you have blocked out time after the meeting, just in case you need it. Again, these may seem small, but they reflect consideration and respect.

- **Set Intentions:** To ensure you have the right mindset before having a tough conversation, it is useful to set intentions. Book at least fifteen minutes in advance of the conversation to settle your mind. Reflect on your values and the values of the organization. What is important in terms of how you believe people should be treated? How do you want to treat other people? Let go of the specifics of what you will say and instead reflect on how you want to show up.

- **Think about the Impact on Others:** Wise leaders know that every action they take has a long shadow. Other people in the organization will pay close attention to how hard situations are managed. Consider in advance what will be communicated to others. Regardless of the reasons, everyone will be looking to see whether the person was treated fairly and with respect. Regardless of the context and the people involved, others may think, "That could be me." Being mindful of the impact of a transition on the people who remain in the organization is critical for their ongoing engagement and motivation.

- **Script the First and the Last Sentence:** Kevin Sneader, global managing partner of McKinsey & Company, shared that his approach to hard conversations includes scripting the first and last sentence. Knowing how you will open and close the conversation helps create "bookends" for the conversation. It also creates space for you to be more authentic during the space in the middle. You can never really know how a conversation will turn, but at least you can know where you want to start and where you want to end.

    Kevin shared with us that the hardest conversations he has occur when he needs to tell one of his colleagues that they did not make senior partner. Every year in June, the firm decides who should be promoted. For each person who makes the cut, three people fall short. Kevin is the one who breaks the bad news. "It is the hardest part of my job," he said. "Harder than business and financial decisions. These are people I've known for many years. Often, they're close friends. They have many outstanding achievements, or they wouldn't have been considered."

Over the years, Kevin has learned that for hard conversations, "one cannot prepare enough. If you're not prepared, you'll be unfocused, and the conversation can go all over the place." But, according to Kevin, finding the right tone requires balance: "Don't prepare too much, or you can then come across as cold and rational." This is the beauty of scripting the first and last sentence: it gives you direction but doesn't make your conversation feel mechanical and detached.

In practice, the objective of the first sentence is to share the bad news. The objective of the last sentence is to keep the line of contact open. In between, the conversation should be driven by the other person: their needs, their questions, their frustrations, and other emotions.

Strategy 2: See Others as Human Beings

Regardless of what the person has done or how you have landed in this difficult conversation, it is imperative to see the other person as a human being. In many cases, the reasons for a termination are clear, but in all situations it is important to remember that you are dealing with human beings. Tips that can be helpful for seeing others as human beings include the following:

- Separate the Action from the Person: We all make mistakes. We all do things we regret. We have all done things that could be seen as "bad," but that does not make us bad people. In engaging in hard conversations, it is helpful to make a clear distinction between what the person did and who the person is. Actions have consequences, but regardless of their actions, people deserve to be treated with kindness and care.

- Widen Your Lens: When approaching a hard conversation, it can be helpful to reflect on the person beyond their role in the organization. Consider what they might be experiencing and who they are outside of work. In many instances, there are extenuating circumstances, such as financial challenges, marital problems, or mental health issues. This broader perspective may not change the outcome of the conversation, but it is a helpful context for expressing greater compassion.

- Don't Be Cruel: In preparing for a hard conversation, it is important to have all the facts. But when giving someone a tough message, it is not necessary to let them know all of the reasons why the decision has been made. Yes, it is important to be prepared with reasons and have data. But once you have delivered the tough message, reminding them of all the things they did wrong or didn't do well enough can add insult to injury. Remember, it is unlikely that you will convince them that you are right. So don't try. Tell them that the decision that has been made and then let them process the information.

Strategy 3: Give People Options

Francine Katsoudas, chief people, policy & purpose officer of Cisco, told us about how she and her team approached a challenge many corporations grappled with in 2020—responding to the economic impact of the Covid-19 pandemic with the least possible impact on their people. While some level of restructuring could not be avoided, Cisco was committed to a highly communicative process with their employees. Cisco had just been ranked number one on the annual "Great Place to Work" list and they returned to a question that had served them well when making previous tough decisions: how should the "greatest place to work" undertake this difficult process in a caring, intentional way? They decided, as Francine told us, to use "a very transparent and empathetic process that gave employees a number of options." People that were already considering a change or retiring were offered a generous severance package should they choose to resign. "Over 2,000 people selected that route," she told us. For others, a dedicated team worked with employees to identify and transition them into other roles within the company, and even worked with some to identify roles outside the company as well. Cisco kept many employees on salary for up to six months while assisting with this placement search within and outside of Cisco. In addition, Francine said, "People could volunteer to take a sabbatical and join a not-for-profit organization for a period of time, keeping their health benefits from Cisco." Laying off people is always difficult, but Cisco committed to an approach driven by care and empathy, one that provided options that would offer additional near-term security and opportunities for career development for as many of their people as possible.

Sometimes there are no "good" options available, but it is still valuable to create opportunities for choice. From a neurological perspective, we don't like situations where we have no control. When we provide options, even if they are not good options, we give people the ability to have some control over what happens. An example of a "not so great" option could be offering them a role that is at a lower compensation level or has less desirable working conditions. In addition we can give people options on whether they would like to share the news with the team or not. Although options will not make the message any easier, it sends a message that you care and want to work together through this process. Providing options gives people a sense of control, even if only in a small way.

Strategy 4: Respond—Don't React

When you inflict pain on other people, they will react. This is a fact. But don't be triggered. Tim Munden, chief learning officer of Unilever, said, "The minute you are triggered, you're in a default reaction and less likely to be compassionate. This is a result of us responding to our own emotions instead of focusing on the person in front of us." Ensuring we remain in the mindset of being responsive, versus being reactive, is critical when engaging in hard conversations.

As shared in chapter 6, mindfulness practice is helpful in enabling us to be more responsive and less reactive. In hard conversations, being able to pause, notice what we are thinking or feeling, and process it without reacting, can help us to not make a challenging situation worse. In a difficult conversation, being able to have this "pause" button can be extremely beneficial.

Strategy 5: Give Time

Giving time during and after a hard conversation can be a gift for all parties. Time offers you space for responding versus reacting, as noted above. It also provides space for people to process what they have heard. Wherever possible, giving people an opportunity to reflect and come back with questions is wise and compassionate. The following are some tips for giving time:

- Be Present: Being present with another person means tuning in to what they are experiencing. In the moment, this may mean sitting in silence with the person, showing them you are not going anywhere. This demonstrates you are there with them in this difficult moment.

- **Plan the Follow-Up:** When someone receives a difficult message, it can be hard for them to process it. Their nervous system can go into a state of shock, a fight-or-flight reaction. Ensuring that you give the person time to process the message, as well as a chance to follow up, is wise and compassionate. Whenever possible, make a plan to follow up. Ensure that the person leaves the meeting knowing they will have time to process your message and be able to come back with questions.

These are all keys to having good hard conversations: be prepared, see others as human beings, give people options, respond instead of reacting, and give time. Let's now look at how to have good feedback conversations.

Good Feedback Conversations

One of the most difficult things we need to do as leaders is provide feedback. Why? Many of us don't like to give feedback because we know it could hurt the other person's feelings. We also fear how they will react: Will they get upset? Will they retaliate?

We are social beings, and one of our greatest fears is being kicked out of the tribe. Getting negative feedback triggers a social pain threat response equal to how we respond to physical pain. This is because we experience social rejection or loss in the same neural network as we experience physical pain.[1]

So, it makes sense that the words "I would like to give you feedback" can activate our fight-flight-freeze response. It is our brain's natural protective mechanism to prepare us for something bad that could threaten our social status or connection to others. But it is not only the recipient of criticism who has the potential to go into survival mode. As has been explored throughout this book, human beings do not like to inflict pain on others. The same neurological wiring that enables us to have empathy and connect with other human beings cautions us against creating harm. We don't like to see other people upset because it will make us feel like a bad person.

This is why most organizations have poor feedback cultures where people don't want to provide it or receive it.

But the only way we can improve and learn is by having candid conversations about things that are not working. So, how can we create conditions whereby we can give and receive feedback in ways that are beneficial to everyone?

Wise compassion is critical.

Wisdom helps us know it is the right thing to do and gives us the courage to speak up. Compassion comes from caring for the human being in front of us and supporting their move past the fear of feedback. Once they do this, they can take advantage of opportunities to learn, adapt, and grow.

In our research, we found that when faced with having to give tough feedback, leaders often end up in Quadrant 1 (Caring Avoidance) or Quadrant 4 (Uncaring Execution). When we care too much, we avoid doing what needs to be done because we don't want to see the other person hurt. Or we give the tough feedback, but we do it in a way that doesn't take into consideration the human being who is receiving it. Both of these approaches have negative outcomes. In Quadrant 1, the individual misses out on an opportunity for growth and improvement. In Quadrant 4, the message is delivered, but the other person may feel angry, hurt, or so put down that they are unable to embrace the opportunity for growth.

There can also be times when we end up in Quadrant 3 (Ineffective Indifference). This includes situations when we give feedback, but don't take into consideration the context. This usually means we've been unskillful in how we delivered the message or were blinded by our biases.

The bottom line is that giving tough feedback is tough, but there are ways we can avoid the pitfalls to support the development of our people. We have identified five strategies that can help.

STRATEGIES FOR GOOD FEEDBACK CONVERSATIONS

- Don't put it off.
- Reframe feedback as a gift.
- Focus on the positive.
- Be objective, not subjective.
- Create a feedback culture.

Let's take a closer look at each of these strategies and how to implement them in a real-world conversation.

Strategy 1: Don't Put It Off

Putting off difficult conversations makes them more difficult. Unlike wine, tough feedback does *not* get better with age. Once you are clear on what needs to be said, there is no benefit to you or to those impacted by delaying the conversation. The more time that passes, the harder it is for people to relate to what you are saying. Delaying the delivery of feedback can also create tension if the person feels something is being left unsaid. The following are a couple of tips to help you avoid the trap of procrastination.

- Keep It Simple: When we distill tough messages into something concrete, clear, and concise, it can make it easier to avoid procrastination. Oftentimes, we procrastinate because we spend too much time thinking about what we will say, how we will say it, and how the other person will react. Although all of these are important considerations, the simpler we can make the message, the easier it is to deliver it sooner. Consider the real issue at hand or what "one thing" would be most valuable for the person to focus on right now. Keeping it simple and focused will not only make it easier to share, but also easier for the other person to receive.

- **Be Less Formal:** Although some feedback needs to be delivered in a formal way, the more we can make feedback informal, the better. For example, say something like "I had some thoughts on the meeting we just had. Is it okay if I share?" Or "It seemed to me that the customer wasn't happy when you said X. Did you notice? And if so, what are your thoughts?" Presented this way, feedback does not need to feel like a big thing but instead becomes a part of how we talk to each other and support each other in learning and growing.

Strategy 2: Reframe Feedback as a Gift

If we are able to see feedback as a gift, it can make it easier to give and receive. Sandra Rivera, chief people officer at Intel, shared with us how she used to see feedback as a "dreaded task that all leaders have to do." Now she sees it as something that is "being offered in the spirit of helping someone grow and succeed, whether in this job or in this company or someplace else." Reframing feedback in this light has made it much easier to provide and also to receive. Some tips that can be helpful to make this shift include the following:

- **Share Because You Care:** Ken Cooper, CHRO of Bloomberg, has a very straightforward view of feedback: "If I am giving you tough feedback, it's because I believe in you and I want to help you improve. If I didn't believe in you, we would be having a different conversation." If we are able to see feedback as a way of saying "I value you, you are important to me and to this organization, and I am willing to invest in your development," it can make it a more positive experience. Note that if you do not believe in the person and are not willing to invest in her or his development, you should be having a different type of conversation.

- **Focus on the Development Opportunity:** In giving tough feedback, we can get caught up in the emotional elements of the conversation. The more we can be specific and focus on tangible, tactical improvement opportunities, the better. Although this varies depending on the situation, if we have the bigger picture in mind—what is core to success in this role or in this company—it can help enhance the quality of the conversation and make it more positively presented and received.

Strategy 3: Focus on the Positive

When we talk about feedback, we immediately assume it is negative. But positive feedback can be incredibly beneficial in terms of motivating us to build on our strengths and learn from tasks we do well. Many of us, however, are not good at giving positive feedback. As human beings we have a negativity bias. We are very good at seeing what went wrong, but not so good at seeing when things are done well. In particular, as leaders, we have developed expertise in seeing what is not working. Often, we have been rewarded for our ability to find faults and fix problems. Nobody has ever been promoted because they were great at noticing "how wonderful we all work together."

So, it is important for us as leaders to train our brain to see the positive and ensure we recognize and acknowledge it. Since this is not natural, it requires intention and effort. Some tips that can be helpful include:

- **Appreciative Inquiry:** Instead of asking "what went wrong?," an appreciative inquiry approach focuses on "how could we have done better?" Because our brains are wired to focus on the negative, it can be beneficial to have an intention to focus on improvements. Even when things don't go well, looking to identify opportunities for people to leverage their strengths can be more motivating than focusing on their deficiencies. In general, an appreciative inquiry mindset helps us train our brains to notice when things go well, so that we remember to recognize and praise those who worked hard to make it happen.

- **Don't Assume They Know:** Leaders can often fall into a trap of assuming that good performers don't need positive feedback. They already know what they do well, right? But this is not always the case. We are often blind to the things we do well because they come more easily to us. Pointing out a strength that is valuable to the organization encourages people to further develop something they are already good at. When we provide thoughtful positive feedback, it shows that we are paying attention. It is a way of saying, "I see you and I appreciate you." We all like to be seen and valued, and it is good to know what is good to do more.

- **Avoid the "Shit" Sandwich:** If the only time we receive positive feedback is when it is delivered before and after we get negative feedback, it loses meaning. Our brains are like Velcro for negative messages and Teflon for positive messages. For this reason, having a formulaic approach to feedback that looks like "positive, negative, positive" can fail because people dismiss the positive and only focus on the negative. Giving positive feedback more often, without tying it to negative feedback, enables people to truly hear what they are doing well. It also helps people to separate things they do well and can enhance from the things they need to develop.

Strategy 4: Be Objective, Not Subjective

It is important to focus on the behavior—on what happened and the resulting impact—not the person. To help remain objective, be sure to distinguish between critical feedback and being critical. When you share a specific example of something you observed and the outcome, you are not making a general comment on the other person's overall ability to do a job. A simple framework for remaining objective is to name the situation, the observed behavior, and the observed outcomes.

As an example, consider the following: "When the client was sharing some of their current challenges, you interrupted to say how we could help. Although I appreciate your intentions, it seemed to me that you made the client feel you were more interested in the sale than in partnering with them to solve their issues."

Strategy 5: Create a Feedback Culture

If we are able to create a culture of candor and transparency, giving feedback can become normalized. Sharing observations of what happened and the outcomes can become how we work together to learn, improve, and develop. Ideally, 80 percent of feedback can be given informally in small, casual ways where we share perspectives and observations, and this becomes part of the culture. The following are some tips on how to create a feedback culture:

- **Ask for Feedback**: Willingly and purposefully ask others to give you feedback. If you as the leader are consistently inquisitive and open to thoughts on your performance, your reports or team members will see feedback as a cultural norm. Seeing it as a norm will make it much easier for people to receive and apply feedback in a meaningful, thoughtful way.

- **Seek Others' Perspectives**: Before narrowing in on what the person did that you feel is not good, consider the context and see if you can view it from another perspective. In any situation, we all have a valid but biased view of what happened—it is never the full story. To help with this, it might also be beneficial to get others' perspectives. It is also important to keep in mind that people don't mess up on purpose. We are all good people who sometimes act in ways that are not beneficial. Seeing other perspectives and understanding the fallibility in all of us is wisdom in action.

- **Be Curious**: Provide the opportunity for others to share their experience. Be curious about their perceptions and why they acted in the way they did. Ask if they agree with your assessment of the negative outcomes, and if they don't, ask why. Be open to learning something new. Perhaps there is another way to see this situation. Seek to gain insight into how they view the world. Ask if they have any suggestions for moving forward. Ask how you can help. And together, create a plan for moving forward.

Practice Does Not Necessarily Make Perfect

When doing hard things in a human way, including having difficult conversations, it's important to remember that we're all human—and humans are unpredictable. Even if you follow all these strategies and give yourself plenty of time to prepare, few hard conversations will go exactly how you hoped or expected. We all process information differently. We all express our emotions differently. But these strategies improve the likelihood that your hardest conversations will go as well as possible both for you and, more important, the person or people you're impacting.

At the end of the day, the best way to ensure a good outcome, whether from a difficult decision or an emotionally painful conversation, is to approach the situation with care and compassion. And the best way to do this is to bring a level of wisdom to each situation. With wisdom, you will be direct and transparent. You will be sensitive to the other person's perspective and treat them the way you would want to be treated. You will put your ego aside and remember that it's about the other person. These are all signs of respect and ways to acknowledge our universal humanity. No matter how difficult a situation or conversation may be, if you come at it from this humanistic position, things will work out as best they can.

You will have, as the chapter title says, come out by going through. And in doing so, you will have enhanced the wisdom and compassion in your leadership and in your organizational culture.

Your Transformation Makes for a More Human World of Work

B ecoming a wise and compassionate leader is a challenging but deeply rewarding process. It is an experience of personal and professional transformation. And it is a lifelong journey. In the many interviews we conducted for this book, a clear pattern emerged. One of our questions was, "Knowing what you know now, what would you have told your younger self?" Nearly all the responses focused on being more courageous earlier to more readily do the hard things of leadership. Rich Lesser, CEO of Boston Consulting Group, put it this way: "One of the lessons I wish I learned when I was younger is to have harder conversations earlier. When I was younger, I was way too cautious. I was either worried I might lose people or worried I would make them unhappy. As I have matured as a leader, I have become better at immediately addressing issues."

This response is both hopeful and informative. It is hopeful because it shows that wise compassionate leadership is effective—that bringing the most human aspects of ourselves into the workplace can raise performance and improve results. It is informative because it reflects the fact that wise compassionate leadership is developed through practice and experience. But it is important to keep in mind that we must be deliberate in this practice. Wise compassionate leadership does not happen unless we put in the effort. Just as musicians and athletes practice their professions, we, too, must practice to become good leaders. As you pay close attention to how you think, speak, and act, with the mission of developing wise compassion, you can gradually shape your character. You can soften your hard edges and transform yourself into a more effective leader.

Be forewarned, though, that practicing wise compassion is not easy. As you've discovered throughout this book, wise compassion can often conflict with our neurological wiring. It sometimes can make us unpopular. And it definitely requires a lot of courage. But hardship and challenges, especially with the people we lead, are worthwhile prices to pay in the journey of becoming a truly great leader. Breakthrough leadership comes from having had many great challenges with the people we lead. Each of these experiences provides us with vital learning and acts as a catalyst to be and do better. In truth, the more challenging or difficult people are, the greater the gift they offer us. This sounds counterintuitive. But in bringing great challenges, other people provide the opportunity for us to strengthen our wisdom and compassion.

Think about this idea for a moment: the people who pose the biggest challenge often provide us the greatest opportunity for our own development and growth. In this way, people provide the critical fuel for us to become compassionate leaders. Nearly every situation is an opportunity to learn. And the more we learn, the better we become. When we experience challenges from the people we work with, we have a choice: we can either resist them or we can see the situation as an opportunity to practice our leadership and our compassion.

Therefore, when people offer you a challenge, welcome it. See it as a gift.

Challenges make you better. They make you work. Avoid pointing fingers or blaming others. Rather, ask yourself what you can learn from the challenge in front of you. Don't pity yourself, and instead see it as another opportunity for lifelong growth. When challenging things happen in relation to other people, train yourself to avoid saying things like "Why did this happen to me, and especially today when I'm so busy?" Instead, begin saying, "Here's a great opportunity for growth. I'm lucky to experience this right now. Even if it takes up a bit of my time, it's time well spent." This is the shift from resistance and avoidance to gratitude and responsiveness.

"Comfort and growth can never coexist," Ginni Rometty, chairwoman and former CEO of IBM, told us. "It's through doing hard and difficult things that you grow and become better. Don't wait until later in your career to make hard decisions. Frontload your career, so these experiences will make you grow and become a great role model for others."

By putting ourselves on the line, facing and embracing hardship, we can transform and develop more wise compassion for others. To really see and understand the perspectives of people, Francine Katsoudas, chief people, policy & purpose officer of Cisco, asked her entire management team to individually have conversations with two people who had just been told they were being let go. She wanted them to connect with people impacted to not only demonstrate that they cared, but to have the opportunity to learn from hearing firsthand about the employees' experience. We learn nothing by trying to avoid the difficulties coming from leading others. If you want to truly grow, you must turn toward, not away from, the opportunities for practice that you are offered. Whenever you experience a challenging situation with another person, ask yourself two questions: "What can I learn from this?" And, "How can I bring kindness and wisdom to this situation?"

Hard Times, Great Hope

Former US president Barack Obama had a plaque on his desk that read, "Hard things are hard." This is an important reminder for all of us. Being a leader is not easy—it's hard. We should remember this so we are not surprised when we face difficult situations and find them challenging. Remembering that leadership is hard helps us to overcome these difficult situations and acknowledge other people's hardships with compassion. If we remember that leadership is hard, we can see leadership as an opportunity to grow into every day, rather than be overwhelmed by it. We lead because people and organizations need leaders, and doing hard things is par for the course.

Consequently, remind yourself every day that challenges and hard decisions are bound to come your way. This may be the single most inevitable aspect of leadership. Challenges are not mistakes. And they are not anyone's fault. No one is to blame. When we acknowledge this reality, we can make necessary decisions in a way that serves the greater good, even when they negatively impact individuals. And we can do it with caring presence, caring courage, caring candor, and caring transparency. The harder the times, the harder the decisions that will need to be made. And the harder the decisions, the bigger the need for making and implementing them in a human way.

In hard times and in hard situations, your impact and your legacy are amplified. For you as a leader, hard situations offer unique opportunities to clearly define and state who you are and what you stand for. Don't squander these chances. Also, keep in mind that any small, kind action will be experienced more strongly during periods of duress than during normal times. Likewise, any unkind action will be amplified. As the impact of your actions is amplified, so is your legacy. You will be best remembered for the decisions you make and the actions you take during difficult times.

There are many reasons to be concerned about the state of the world. But there are also compelling reasons to be optimistic. We at Potential Project have a unique vantage point for observing the state of individuals, organizations, countries, and the world. Through our work with leaders of companies and public organizations, we see a massive global movement. This movement includes an increase in human, social, and environmental responsibility. It includes the incorporation of purpose and strong values as part of taking action.

It is a movement of wise and compassionate leadership.

Embracing the challenge of becoming a wise compassionate leader is an urgent calling. The fact that you, like thousands of other leaders, are reading this book now shows there is much good in the world—and this goodness is gaining momentum. We are confident humankind will make the changes needed to improve our world, our societies, and our organizations. But we also know this will require the effort of every single person capable of influencing others through wisdom and compassion. You've already shown your commitment to this change. We hope this book has provided you with the inspiration and the tools to be an even bigger part of creating a more human world of work.

Compassionate Leadership

Research Methodology and Background

At Potential Project, we are research-led. With innovative and industry-leading diagnostic tools and in partnership with academics from leading universities, we look for the data that tells stories and patterns that unlock insights. Our proprietary research studies reveal a future of work that is truly human-centric.

The data shared in this book is from two of our proprietary assessment tools: Compassionate Leader Assessment and Mindgrow. Both of these assessments are tools we use for research purposes, as well as with our clients to enhance understanding of their people and culture. In this appendix, we provide information on both of these assessments and the specific data collected and analyzed for this book.

Compassionate Leadership Assessment

The Compassionate Leadership Assessment was developed in partnership with academic researchers at Harvard Business School,

Columbia Business School, Haas School of Business at the University of California at Berkeley, Rotman School of Management at the University of Toronto, and the University of Amsterdam School of Business.

It is designed to assess leaders on their level of compassion and their level of wisdom. We define compassion as having the intention to be of benefit to others. It is assessed in contrast to indifference. We define wisdom as knowing the right thing to do and having the courage to do it. It is assessed in contrast to ignorance.

Participants in the assessment were recruited in collaboration with the *Harvard Business Review* through a published article on compassionate leadership. Research participation was completely voluntary and anonymous.

Overview of Participants

A total of 2,038 leaders took part in the assessment.

- 63% female and 37% male
- Average age is 46 years.
- Participants hold a variety of leadership positions:
  - 19% identified as staff or team leaders
  - 26% as middle managers
  - 19% as upper managers
  - 12% as senior directors
  - 26% as executive leaders
- Participants represent a range of different industries:
  - Health care (15%, 305 respondents)
  - Technology (14%, 285 respondents)
  - Professional services and consulting (11%, 224 respondents)

- – Government and public services (11%, 224 respondents)
- – Consumer products and retail (6%, 122 respondents)
- – Telecom and media (3%, 61 respondents)
- – Banking and capital markets (3%, 61 respondents)
- – Industrial products and construction (3%, 61 respondents)
- – Insurance (2%, 40 respondents)
- – Oil and gas (2%, 40 respondents)
- – Life sciences (2%, 40 respondents)
- – Power and utilities (1%, 20 respondents)
- – Automotive (1%, 20 respondents)
- – "Other" not identified (25%, 509 respondents)
- Participants represent a range of different company sizes:
  - – Under 100 employees (32%)
  - – 100 to 1,000 employees (25%)
  - – 1,000 to 5,000 employees (15%)
  - – 5,000 to 10,000 employees (7%)
  - – 10,000 to 100,000 employees (15%)
  - – Over 100,000 employees (6%)
- Most participants are from North America (62%), followed by Europe (17%) and Asia (12%).

Data Collected

The assessment collected demographic information and participants' self-reported attitudes (stress, intention to quit, burnout, etc.). Compassion was measured using a thirty-item scale developed specifically for this research.

After completing the assessment, participants were invited to ask their direct reports to provide feedback on their leadership. No identifiable data about direct reports was collected. Leader and direct report responses were linked using a unique identifier, which was automatically generated in the back end of the survey system.

A total of 999 direct reports completed the survey. On average, each participant was rated by 6.1 direct reports (minimum 1, maximum 36).

Statistical analyses and models were run by measuring (1) leaders' self-ratings, (2) direct reports' other-ratings (of the participant leaders), and (3) the extent of difference between self- and other-ratings.

Mindgrow

Mindgrow was built, tested, and validated in close collaboration with a *Fortune* 500 global consultancy and in partnership with academic researchers at Harvard Business School, Columbia Business School, Haas School of Business at the University of California at Berkeley, and the Rotman School of Management at the University of Toronto.

Mindgrow is a digital diagnostic tool that reveals the hidden side of the mind at work. It helps the user understand how daily focus and emotional experiences drive peak productivity and wellness while at work.

Unlike typical survey tools, Mindgrow accompanies users during their workday, releasing prompts at random points in the day and asking a series of tailored questions. In doing so, Mindgrow tracks a person's mindsets, attitudes, and behaviors on a momentary basis during the workday and workweek.

Also, Mindgrow applies user experience and gamification principles to encourage active involvement from participants. Individuals are incentivized through a game-style play that rewards participation and fast response times.

Participants in Mindgrow were recruited through a published article with *Forbes* and *Harvard Business Review* on mind wandering at work. Research participation was completely voluntary and anonymous.

Overview of Participants

A total of 2,143 people took part in Mindgrow, resulting in a total of 225,000 individual observations.

- 54% female and 46% male

- Average age is 42 years.

- Participants hold a variety of leadership positions:
  - 28% identified as staff or team leaders
  - 17% as middle managers
  - 19% as upper managers
  - 11% as senior directors
  - 25% as executive leaders

- Participants represent a range of different industries:
  - Health care (5%)
  - Technology (11%)
  - Professional services and consulting (41%)
  - Government and public services (8%)

- Participants represent a range of different company sizes:
  - Under 100 employees (30%)
  - 100 to 1,000 employees (27%)
  - 1,000 to 5,000 employees (11%)

- 5,000 to 10,000 employees (9%)
- 10,000 to 100,000 employees (17%)
- Over 100,000 employees (6%)
- Most participants are from Europe (42%), followed by North America (26%), Asia (15%), and Australia (10%).

Data Collected

During the onboarding part of the diagnostic, Mindgrow collected demographic information and information about participants' work style and personality.

For the five days of the Mindgrow diagnostic, participants received three notifications throughout the day—morning, midday, and mid- to late afternoon. At these points, information was gathered on mind-wandering, stressor(s) experienced, daily resilience, task concentration and distraction, task meaning, emotional functioning, sleep quality, hours worked, work location, and mindfulness practice.

At the end of the diagnostic period, a final assessment collected information on job engagement, job satisfaction, burnout, organizational commitment, leadership support, meaning in work, compassion, and mindfulness.

ACKNOWLEDGMENTS

When we set out on this journey, we knew it would be beneficial to collect stories from voices of experience. We are truly grateful to all the leaders who shared their insights and experiences with us. Although we were not able to include a story or quote from every person we interviewed, we have worked to share the collective wisdom from all. We are inspired and appreciative of every leader we spoke with and their ongoing efforts to do "hard things in a human way."

We also knew that with a seemingly "soft" topic like compassion, it would be important to back things up with research and data. We are so fortunate to have an incredible research team who supported our efforts and never flinched when we asked for "just one more thing." Thank you, Nick Hobson, Darja Kragt, Leandra McIntosh, Kimiko Davis, and Jason Beck. We are also grateful to our research partners including: Jennifer Chatman from Haas School of Business; Sandra Matz from Columbia Business School; Joanna Sosnwska from University of Amsterdam; Michael Inzlicht from University of Toronto; Juliana Schroeder from Haas School of Business; and Ashley Whillans from Harvard Business School.

Beyond our research team, we are grateful to all our amazing colleagues at Potential Project who directly or indirectly supported us in this book. In particular, we would like to thank our other partners and our leadership team for having our backs and providing insights, including Rob Stembridge, Erick Rinner, Paula Kelley, Christel Leonhard, and Jenni Elise Toulson. We would also like to acknowledge the team who dedicated countless hours behind the scenes helping to contact leaders, coordinate interviews, review drafts, and keep us organized, including Shannon Jordan, Jennifer Kim, Matilda Havsteen, Omar Qarwan, and Marta Hankiewicz. We are also deeply grateful to our network of highly skilled facilitators who share ideas and bring our programs to life.

We have been blessed by incredible editorial support by Jeff Leeson of Benson Collister. Jeff's commitment to clarity and simplicity has helped distill complex matter into clear insights. We are also grateful to our agent, Jim Levine of Levine Greenberg Rostan Literary Agency, whose dedication to our work has been a driving force behind the process. We would also like to acknowledge our editor, Jeff Kehoe from Harvard Business Review Press. Jeff is passionate about bringing the practices of this book to leaders and has been a champion throughout. We are also deeply grateful to the whole team at Harvard Business Review Press for our ongoing partnership, including Jeff Kehoe, Sally Ashworth, Julie Devoll, Adi Ignatius, and many more.

We are also deeply grateful to the mind training masters who have guided us in this work and supported us in our own inner journeys. Our teachers include the Dalai Lama, Lama Zopa Rinpoche, Mingyur Rinpoche, Alan Wallace, Roshi Joan Halifax, Matthieu Ricard, Stephan Pende, Glen Svensson, and the Venerable Sangye Khadro.

And finally, this book would not have been possible without the love and support of our families. We are truly blessed to be surrounded by partners, parents, siblings, children, and pets who provide us with the encouragement and space to do this work. You know who you are, and we love you all very much.

NOTES

Introduction

1. Additional information on our research methods and partners can be found in the appendix.

2. O. Torrès, "The Silent and Shameful Suffering of Bosses: Layoffs in SME," *International Journal of Entrepreneurship and Small Business* 13 (2011): 181–192.

Chapter 1

1. T. Allas and B. Schaninger, "The Boss Factor: Making the World a Better Place through Workplace Relations," *McKinsey Quarterly*, September 22, 2020.

2. B. Hare and V. Woods, *Survival of the Friendliest: Understanding Our Origins and Rediscovering Our Common Humanity* (New York: Penguin Random House, 2020).

3. P. Ekman, "Darwin's Compassionate View of Human Nature," *JAMA* 303 (2010): 557–558.

4. C. Darwin, *The Descent of Man: And Selection in Relation to Sex* (London: John Murray, 1871).

5. Ekman, "Darwin's Compassionate View of Human Nature," 557–558.

6. Ji-Woong Kim et al., "Compassionate Attitude towards Others' Suffering Activates the Mesolimbic Neural System," *Neuropsychologia* 47 (2009): 2073–2081.

7. C. De Dreu and M. Kret, "Oxytocin Conditions Intergroup Relations through Upregulated In-Group Empathy, Cooperation, Conformity, and Defense," *Biological Psychiatry* 79 (2016): 165–173.

8. L. L. Lengersdorff et al., "When Implicit Prosociality Trumps Selfishness: The Neural Valuation System Underpins More Optimal Choices When Learning to Avoid Harm to Others Than to Oneself," *Journal of Neuroscience* 40 (2020): 7286–7299; J. Rilling et al., "A Neural Basis for Social Cooperation," *Neuron* 35 (2002): 395–405.

9. C. Leonardo et al., "Increasing Generosity by Disrupting Prefrontal Cortex," *Social Neuroscience* 12 (2017): 174–181.

10. D. Kahneman and A. Deaton, "High Income Improves Evaluation of Life but Not Emotional Well-Being," *Proceedings of the National Academy of Sciences of the United States of America* 107 (2010): 16489–16493; K. G. Denny and H. Steiner, "External and Internal Factors Influencing Happiness in Elite Collegiate Athletes," *Child Psychiatry and Human Development* 40 (2009): 55–72.

Chapter 2

1. J. E. Dutton et al., "Compassion at Work," *Annual Review of Organizational Psychology and Organizational Behavior* 1 (March 2014): 277–304.

2. J. A. Clair et al., "This Is How We Do It: How Perceived Prosocial Impact Offsets Negative Personal Outcomes Associated with Carrying Out Necessary Evils," *Journal of Management Inquiry* 25, no. 3 (2016): 301–321.

3. S. Mittal and K. Deb, "Optimal Strategies of the Iterated Prisoner's Dilemma Problem for Multiple Conflicting Objectives," *IEEE Transactions on Evolutionary Computation* 13 (2009): 554–565; M. L. Locey and H. Rachlin, "Commitment and Self-Control in a Prisoner's Dilemma Game," *Journal of the Experimental Analysis of Behavior* 98 (2012): 89–103.

4. B. M. Zagorsky et al., "Forgiver Triumphs in Alternating Prisoner's Dilemma," *PloS One* 8 (2013): 80814; T. Yamagishi et al., "Separating Trust from Cooperation in a Dynamic Relationship: Prisoner's Dilemma with Variable Dependence," *Rationality and Society* 17, no. 3 (2005): 275–308.

5. Business Roundtable, "Business Roundtable Redefines the Purpose of a Corporation to Promote 'an Economy That Serves All Americans,'" August 2019, https://www.businessroundtable.org/business-roundtable-redefines-the-purpose-of-a-corporation-to-promote-an-economy-that-serves-all-americans.

6. A. Gorsky, quoted in "Business Roundtable Redefines the Purpose of a Corporation."

7. L. Fink, "A Fundamental Reshaping of Finance," *BlackRock*, January 2020, https://www.blackrock.com/us/individual/larry-fink-ceo-letter.

Chapter 3

1. D. Goleman, R. E. Boyatzis, and A. McKee, *Primal Leadership: Unleashing the Power of Emotional Intelligence* (Boston: Harvard Business Review Press, 2013).

2. O. M. Klimecki et al., "Differential Pattern of Functional Brain Plasticity after Compassion and Empathy Training," *Social Cognitive and Affective Neuroscience* 9 (2014): 873–879.

3. Klimecki et al., "Differential Pattern of Functional Brain Plasticity," 873–879.

4. H. G. Engen and T. Singer, "Empathy Circuits," *Current Opinion in Neurobiology* 23 (2013): 275–282.

5. K. Ahola et al., "Burnout as a Predictor of All-Cause Mortality among Industrial Employees: A 10-Year Prospective Register-Linkage Study," *Journal of Psychosomatic Research* 69 (2010): 51–57.

6. Klimecki et al., "Differential Pattern of Functional Brain Plasticity," 873–879.

7. Hare and Woods, *Survival of the Friendliest*.

8. E. N. Simas et al., "How Empathic Concern Fuels Political Polarization," *American Political Science Review* 114 (2019): 258–269.

9. P. Bloom, "Empathy and Its Discontents," *Trends in Cognitive Sciences* 21 (2017): 24–31.

Chapter 4

1. R. Hougaard and J. Carter, *The Mind of the Leader: How to Lead Yourself, Your People, and Your Organization for Extraordinary Results* (Boston: Harvard Business Review Press, 2018).

2. K. D. Williams and S. A. Nida, "Ostracism: Consequences and Coping," *Current Directions in Psychological Science* 20, no. 2 (2011): 71–75.

3. R. F. Baumeister and M. R. Leary, "The Need to Belong: Desire for Interpersonal Attachments as a Fundamental Human Motivation," *Psychological Bulletin* 117 (1995): 497–529.

4. M. Sarkar and D. Fletcher, "Ordinary Magic, Extraordinary Performance: Psychological Resilience and Thriving in High Achievers," *Sport, Exercise, and Performance Psychology* 3 (2014): 46–60.

5. K. Neff, "The Motivational Power of Self-Compassion," *Self-Compassion*, May 2011, https://self-compassion.org/the-motivational-power-of-self-compassion/.

6. K. Neff, "Why Self-Compassion Is Healthier Than Self-Esteem," *Self-Compassion*, June 2011, https://self-compassion.org/why-self-compassion-is -healthier-than-self-esteem/.

Chapter 5

1. J. M. Darley and C. D. Batson, "From Jerusalem to Jericho: A Study of Situational and Dispositional Variables in Helping Behavior," *Journal of Personality and Social Psychology* 27 (1973): 100–108.

2. M. Kivimäki et al., "Long Working Hours and Risk of Coronary Heart Disease and Stroke: A Systematic Review and Meta-analysis of Published and Unpublished Data for 603,838 Individuals," *Lancet* 386 (2015): 1739–1746.

3. S. Bellezza et al., "Conspicuous Consumption of Time: When Busyness and Lack of Leisure Time Become a Status Symbol," *Journal of Consumer Research* 44 (2014): 118–138.

4. H. Bruch and S. Ghoshal, "Beware the Busy Manager," *Harvard Business Review*, February 2002, pp. 62–69, https://hbr.org/2002/02/beware-the-busy-manager.

5. J. Birkinshaw and J. Cohen, "Make Time for the Work That Matters," *Harvard Business Review*, September 2013, pp. 2–5, https://hbr.org/2013/09/make -time-for-the-work-that-matters.

6. P. A. Atroszko and B. Atroszko, "The Costs of Work-Addicted Managers in Organizations: Towards Integrating Clinical and Organizational Frameworks," *Amfiteatru Economic* 22, no. 14 (2020): 1265–1282.

7. S. Kurczy, "Embracing Busyness," Columbia Business School, May 2018, https://www8.gsb.columbia.edu/articles/ideas-work/embracing-busyness.

8. S. Kurczy, "Embracing Busyness."

9. M. Hansen, *Great at Work: How Top Performers Do Less, Work Better, and Achieve More* (New York: Simon and Schuster, 2018).

10. Vanity Fair, "Apple's Jony Ive Full Conversation with Graydon Carter," June 2020, https://www.youtube.com/watch?v=ef69BUlge-A.

Chapter 6

1. J. Roberts and M. E. David, "Put Down Your Phone and Listen to Me: How Boss Phubbing Undermines the Psychological Conditions Necessary for Employee Engagement," *Computers in Human Behavior* 75 (2017): 206–217.

2. M. A. Killingsworth and D. T. Gilbert, "A Wandering Mind Is an Unhappy Mind," *Science* 330 (2010): 932.

3. Killingsworth and Gilbert, "A Wandering Mind."

4. M. Pollan, *How to Change Your Mind: What the New Science of Psychedelics Teaches Us about Consciousness, Dying, Addiction, Depression, and Transcendence* (New York: Penguin Random House, 2018).

5. K. A. Garrison et al., "Meditation Leads to Reduced Default Mode Network Activity beyond an Active Task," *Cognitive, Affective, Behavioral Neuroscience* 15 (2015): 712–720.

6. P. Croce, S. Covey, and B. Lyon, *Lead or Get Off the Pot! The Seven Secrets of a Self-Made Leader* (New York: Touchstone, 2004), p. 14.

7. D. Kahneman, *Thinking Fast and Slow* (New York: Farrar, Straus and Giroux, 2011).

8. A. Chiesa, A. Serretti, and J. C. Jakobsen, "Mindfulness: Top-Down or Bottom-Up Emotion Regulation Strategy?," *Clinical Psychology Review* 33 (2013): 82–96; F. Zeidan, "The Neurobiology of Mindfulness Meditation," in *Handbook of Mindfulness: Theory, Research, and Practice*, ed. K. W. Brown, J. D. Creswell, and R. M. Ryan (New York: Guilford Press, 2015), pp. 171–189.

9. Y. Y. Tang et al., "Improving Executive Function and Its Neurobiological Mechanisms through a Mindfulness-Based Intervention: Advances within the Field of Developmental Neuroscience," *Child Development Perspectives* 6 (2012): 361–366.

Chapter 7

1. J. Bardwick, *Danger in the Comfort Zone: From Boardroom to Mailroom— How to Break the Entitlement Habit That's Killing American Business* (New York: AMACOM, 1995).

2. B. Brown, *Dare to Lead: Brave Work. Tough Conversations. Whole Hearts* (New York: Penguin Random House, 2018).

3. B. Brown, "The Power of Vulnerability," TED Talk, January 2011, https://www.ted.com/talks/brene_brown_the_power_of_vulnerability/transcript.

4. D. Goleman and R. E. Boyatzis, "Emotional Intelligence Has 12 Elements. Which Do You Need to Work On?," *Harvard Business Review*, February 6, 2017, https://hbr.org/2017/02/emotional-intelligence-has-12-elements-which-do-you-need -to-work-on.

5. Brown, *Dare to Lead*.

6. B. T. Litz, "Emotional Numbing in Combat-Related Post-Traumatic Stress Disorder: A Critical Review and Reformulation," *Clinical Psychology Review* 12 (1992): 417–432.

Chapter 8

1. E. Meyer, *The Culture Map: Breaking through the Invisible Boundaries of Global Business* (New York: PublicAffairs, 2014).

Chapter 9

1. C. Duhigg, "What Google Learned from Its Quest to Build the Perfect Team," *New York Times Magazine*, February 28, 2016, https://www.nytimes.com /2016/02/28/magazine/what-google-learned-from-its-quest-to-build-the-perfect -team.html.

2. M. Frazier et al., "Psychological Safety: A Meta-Analytic Review and Extension," *Personnel Psychology* 70 (2017): 113–165.

3. N. Shahinpoor and B. F. Matt, "The Power of One: Dissent and Organizational Life," *Journal of Business Ethics* 74 (2007): 37–48.

4. M. B. Nielsen et al., "Authentic Leadership and Its Relationship with Risk Perception and Safety Climate," *Leadership and Organization Development Journal* 34 (2013): 308–325.

Chapter 10

1. N. Eisenberger, "The Neural Bases of Social Pain: Evidence for Shared Representations with Physical Pain," *Psychosomatic Medicine* 74, no. 2 (2012): 126–135.

INDEX

Note: Figures are identified by *f* following the page number.

ABOUT THE AUTHORS

RASMUS HOUGAARD is the founder and CEO of Potential Project and the coauthor of the groundbreaking book by Harvard Business Review Press, *The Mind of the Leader: How to Lead Yourself, Your People, and Your Organization for Extraordinary Results*. Rasmus was nominated by Thinkers50 as one of the eight most important leadership thinkers in the world today. He writes for *Harvard Business Review, Forbes*, and *Business Insider*. He is a sought-after keynote speaker and leadership developer who coaches and supports C-suite executives at global organizations such as IKEA, Accenture, Cisco, and Unilever.

JACQUELINE CARTER is a partner and North American Director for Potential Project. She is recognized globally for developing the innate potential of leaders and organizations, as well as for her dynamic presentation skills and thoughtful publications. She works with leading organizations including Cisco, Accenture, Disney, and Danaher. Jacqueline is the coauthor of *The Mind of the Leader: How to Lead Yourself, Your People, and Your Organization for Extraordinary Results* and *One Second Ahead: Enhance Your Performance at Work with Mindfulness*. She is a regular contributor to *Harvard Business Review, Forbes, Leader to Leader, Mindful Magazine*, and *Business Insider*.

MARISSA AFTON is a partner and Head of Global Accounts for Potential Project. As a driving force behind leadership development and change initiatives at multinational organizations, Marissa helps leaders and organizations to unlock their potential to create cultural excellence and superior performance, resilience, and innovation.

She has worked with leading companies including Cisco, Eli Lilly, Varian, and White & Case. Recognized for her breadth of knowledge and deep experience in transforming organizations by transforming the mind, Marissa is also a sought-after global speaker and contributor to publications such as *Harvard Business Review.*

MOSES MOHAN is the Head of Leadership Solutions for Potential Project. A multidisciplinary maverick with roles traversing multiple domains, including coach, consultant, designer, facilitator, and Zen monk, Moses brings a unique blend of expertise in strategy, transformation, and contemplative training in teams and organizations. He partners with leading organizations such as Accenture, IKEA, and Unilever to drive systemic interventions that unleash human potential at scale and coaches leaders to transform themselves, their teams, and their organizations to unlock breakthrough performance. He is a regular contributor on topics at the intersection of ancient wisdom, leadership, and behavioral science in platforms such as *Forbes* and *Harvard Business Review.*

Potential Project is a global research, leadership development, and consulting firm on a mission to create a more human world of work. We help individuals, leaders, and teams to uncover the power of the mind and to unlock positive, sustainable change. For more than a decade, we have helped thousands of individuals at more than 500 clients to adopt new ways of working and leading. We are present in 28 countries with a network of over 200 consultants and facilitators, and we serve hundreds of forward-thinking companies like IKEA, Unilever, Cisco, LEGO, and Accenture. For more information, go to www.potentialproject.com.

If you are interested in further exploring the topic of compassionate leadership, we invite you to visit www.compassionateleadershipbook .com. You will find both inspiration and practical tips and approaches for building compassion into your own leadership, along with information about upcoming leadership events, including exclusive learning webinars and in-person immersive retreats.

This book has come to life through our work and conversations with thousands of leaders around the world. If you have comments, questions, or experiences to share about the practices in this book and your leadership journey, please email us at rasmus.hougaard@potentialproject.com or jacqueline.carter@potentialproject.com. While we may not be able to respond to all messages, we would love to hear from you.